The Mystery Fancier

Volume 6, Number 2
March/April 1982

The Mystery Fancier

Volume 6, Number 2
March/April 1982

TABLE OF CONTENTS

The Mystery Fancier
(USPS: 428-590)
is edited and published bi-monthly by
Guy M. Townsend
1711 Clifty Drive
Madison, IN 47250

SUBSCRIPTION RATES: Domestic second class mail, $12.00 per year (6 is-
sues); overseas surface mail, $12.00; overseas airmail, $18.00. Overseas subscribers pleas pay in international money order, check drawn
on U.S. bank, or currency; no checks drawn of foreign banks, please.
Single copy price: $2.50

Second class postage paid at Madison, Indiana.

ISBN: 978-1-4344-3630-6

WILDSIDE PRESS

Mysteriously Speaking . . .

I'm afraid that I'm going to take up much more of this issue than is my wont. Instead of my normal one or two pages of
blather, I'm going to run on for six full pages before I start
skipping around and filling in the blank spaces at the ends of
the various articles and departments. All of a sudden, after
a long period of relative quiescence, I find that I have a
great deal to say. And, as this introductory apology only
compounds the problem for which I am apologizing, I'll cut it
short now and get right into the first order of business.

REPRINTING VOLUME ONE OF THE MYSTERY FANCIER

Actually, it's just an idea so far. I need to know what
you people think before I go ahead with it. First, a little
history. (Bear with me, folks. This is one of my longer
stories.) *The Mystery Fancier* got its start back in November
1976 with an unnumbered "Preview Issue." That 42-page magazine was mimeographed on blue, 8½" x 11" pages and was stapled
along one side. The next two issues (TMF 1:1 [January 1977]
and 1:2 [March 1977]) were printed in the same manner and on
the same paper and were 48 and 56 pages long, respectively.
Why blue paper, you wonder? Well, the mimeograph process lays
down a much heavier layer of ink than does the offset process,
and mimeo paper absorbs much more ink than does offset bond;
as a result, the type on one side of a mimeographed sheet can
sometimes be read from the other side, *through* the paper.
This, obviously, is a drawback, and one way of getting around
it is to use colored paper whose own darkness reduces the
show-through. Now you know. Even with the blue paper, I was
still getting some show-through, so with TMF 1:3 (May 1977, 58
pp.) I switched to a much darker paper, the color of which, if
I remember correctly, was officially designated "lilac." Whatever it was called, it was sure as hell dark, and it solved
the show-through problem nicely. Unfortunately, it was also
highly conducive to eye-strain, so I stopped using it (and
colored paper altogether) after TMF 1:4 (July 1977, 60 pp.).
TMF 1:4 was notable not only for being the last of the
colored TMFs, but also for being the first in the new, saddle-
stapled, digest size. For that change, the blame--or perhaps
the credit--is directly attributable to the post office. I
had mailed out the first few issues via book-rate mail, but

1

when I took TMF 1:3 to the post office I was informed that it did not qualify for fourth-class mailing. I managed to sneak that issue through (by mailing it at a different post office), but, since I couldn't afford to mail out a large magazine at first-class rates, I had to find some way to mail the magazine without putting myself even further in the red than I already was. In the end, I decided to reduce the physical size of the magazine without reducing its content and then mail the smaller publication first class.

To do this, I used a handy little machine which I had acquired at the same time that I purchased my mimeograph machine. (Did I mention that I was doing my own printing back in those days? Well, I was.) It was called an electronic stencil cutter, and what it did was enable me to bypass the hassle of typing stencils. All issues through TMF 1:3 had been typed directly on stencils, which is a maddening task for someone, like myself, inclined to make more than his fair shares of typos. Correcting stencils, for those of you fortunate enough to have escaped that torturous chore, requires rolling up the stencil, applying a layer of correction fluid, waiting a minute to let it dry, rolling the stencil back to where it was, and then typing in the correct letter. A mere handful of mistakes per page can easily add ten minutes to the time it takes to type a single stencil. With the electronic stencil cutter, however, the copy is typed on ordinary typing paper, which is much easier to make corrections on (especially if you have a correcting Selectric), and then is transferred to the stencil by the electronic stencil cutter. Since I wanted to get as many words as possible on each page, I added the extra step of having my copy reduced before transferring it to the stencil.

The results were mixed. I got more words to the page, but the readability was nothing to write home about. Electronic stencil cutters produce images that are more fuzzy than those produced by regular stencils, and the fuzziness combined with the reduced size and the purple paper to make TMF 1:4 a real eye-ball bruiser. As I said, I abandoned the colored paper after TMF 1:4, but TMF 1:5 (September 1977, 60 pp.) and 1:6 (November 1977, 60 pp.) were still afflicted with small, fuzzy, difficult-to-read type. (In fact, it wasn't until TMF 2:4 [July 1978] that TMF switched from mimeo to offset printing, and once again the post office was the cause of the change: I decided to get a second-class mailing permit, and mimeographed publications cannot be sent second class.)

From this run-down you can see that volume one of TMF had a peculiar history; what it *didn't* have was a lot of subscribers. Only about fifty people wrote for copies of the Preview Issue when I was giving them away back in 1976, and I think the subscription roll still numbered fewer than a hundred at the end of the first year. I didn't run off many extra copies, so the first volume of TMF was quickly out of print. Newcomers frequently asked me to reprint the early issues, but there never seemed to be enough of a demand to make it worthwhile. Recently, however, several things have happened to make me reconsider. First, TMF's circulation has increased dramatically over the past year, having passed the four-hundred mark if you include bookstore sales, and the great majority of current readers have never even seen copies of the early issues. Second, when I offered a used set of volume one plus the Preview Issue for auction last year, seventeen people entered bids of

from $15 to $50 dollars, and the winner, Harry Dashoff, had
the grace to write to me after he received the magazines and
say, "I consider it a bargain!"

The third reason I am thinking about reissuing volume one
will require more explanation. It has, indirectly, to do with
Brownstone Books. As most of you know, several bibliographies
of crime fiction criticism have been published over the past
couple of years. (The best of these is Jon Breen's splendid
but regrettably short *What About Murder?*, which I consider a
dead cert for an Edgar this year.) However, none of these
bibliographies is comprehensive, and there is still a crying
need for a definitive, annotated, world bibliography of crime
fiction criticism.

That need is about to be met. Walter Albert, who has for
years done an annual bibliography for *The Armchair Detective*,
is hard at work on a bibliography that will cover the field
more comprehensively than any other work to date. It will,
for example, cover, with full annotations, works in all the
major languages of the world. And, more to the point, it will
cover the contents of mystery fanzines, which have largely
been neglected by bibliographical studies other than Walter's
TAD articles.

What has this to do with reprinting volume one of TMF?
Just this: there's not much point in drawing a researcher's
attention to, say, Art Scott's two articles on Harry Stephen
Keeler in TMF One if that researcher can't lay his hands on
the relevant issues. For this reason, Walter and his associates (he's not doing this alone) are including in their work
an appendix listing places where runs of the various magazines
can be found. When I was asked to check back over my old subscription rolls and provide a list of libraries which have
been with TMF from the beginning, I was embarrassed to have to
say that there were, at best, only two such places on earth,
and I wasn't really sure about them. Soon thereafter I received queries about back issues from two university libraries,
and these queries provided the impetus which finally got me to
thinking about reprinting TMF One. (Not to leave you hanging
on a limb, Walter's bibliography will be published by Brownstone Books, this year we hope, and I'll be sure to keep you
posted.)

If I am going to reprint these early issues--and that's
still a big if--then I may as well up the quality of them
somewhat and at the same time give a belated but (I hope)
nonetheless welcome response to the complaints of those who
felt put out by the mid-volume change in format. The Preview
Issue and the first three issues of TMF were mimeographed from
cut stencils which I did not save, so the reprints will have
to be made from my file copies of the issues. I have discovered, rather to my surprise, that it is possible to make
photocopies of these colored pages on which the background
color is totally eliminated, so using photocopies to print
from should solve part of the readability problem. Second,
since I'll not be tied to using the original stencils, there's
no reason why I can't have these early issues reduced to the
same digest size that went into effect with 1:4, which will
enable those who so desire to bind all of the issues of TMF
One into a single volume uniform with all later volumes. That
should solve the format-change problem. All that then remains
is the problem of fuzziness on the reduced copy in numbers

four through six. As it happens, I still have the original
dypescripts for those numbers, and I can print directly from
those pages and produce results equivalent to what you now
hold in your hand. And that should solve the fuzziness
problem.

In short, if there is sufficient interest to justify the
expense, I can produce individual reprints of the first seven
numbers (the Preview Issue and the six issues of volume one)
in a uniform format with copy more readable than in the originals. The question is: Is there sufficient interest? The
cost would largely be determined by the number of people who
are interested. If all of TMF's current subscribers bought
copies of the reprints, they could be priced at the current
subscription rate--$2.00 per copy, for a total of $14.00 for
the set of seven issues. But we all know that not all current
subscribers are going to want copies. A lot of them already
have the originals, and a lot of others just aren't interested
in non-current fanzines. In all likelihood, the demand will
be small, and if it is too small the per-unit cost will be too
high to justify going through with it. At a guess, I would
say that $20.00 is about the highest price that could reason-
ably be expected to fly, so let me put it to you this way:
Would you be willing to pay $20.00 for a set of the first
seven issues of *The Mystery Fancier*, offset printed and produced in a format uniform with the issue you are not reading?
If you would be, drop me a postcard to that effect. When I
see how many of you are interested, I can find out whether it
will be practical to go ahead with the reprinting. Don't say
yes unless you really mean it--I'd hate to invest money in
this project and then have a lot of you tell me that you've
changed your minds. If you'll respond quickly, I may be able
to let you know by the next issue of TMF whether the reprint
project is on, and if it *is* on I should be able to get the
reprints to you by early summer. Let me hear from you.

TWO NEW PUBLICATIONS

Moving on, at last, to other matters, there are a couple
of new publications to which I would like to call your attention. The first is *Mystery News*. In a letter addressed "Dear
Mystery Readers" in the January/February 1982 issue of this
16-page tabloid, editor Patricia Shnell writes:

> Our primary purpose in publishing *Mystery News* is to tell you
> about as many new mystery books, those recently published and
> those about to be published, as possible. Demand for mysteries,
> in all categories, has never been greater, and publishers are
> responding by announcing expansion of their mystery lines. But
> promotion budgets for individual titles will probably not in-
> crease, so fans will not be aware of how many new books are
> available. We hope to bring you letters from, and interviews
> with, some of the authors who have books mentioned in the same
> issue of *Mystery News*, and dates and locations of their personal
> appearances and autograph parties. We will invite editors to
> tell us about their new mystery lines and what they project for
> us in the immediate future. There will be reviews too, by people
> who enjoy the kind of mystery they are reading, and are knowledge-
> able about the mechanics of writing.

The single-copy price is $1.95, and a year's subscription (six issues) is $9.95. Canadian and Mexican subscribers must pay an additional $4.50; overseas subscribers must pay an additional $9.60. The address is *Mystery News*, P.O. Box 3750, Sparks, NV 89431.

Then there's *The Dossier*, "The Official Journal of the International Spy Society." It is a slick publication with impressive artwork (graphics and photos), pleasing typesetting, and contents sure to set the spy aficionado's heart a pounding. A year's subscription (four issues) can be had by sending a check for $12.00, made payable to The International Spy Society, to Richard L. Knudson, Editor, *The Dossier*, State University of New York, English Department, Oneonta, NY 13820. The price of a single copy is $4.00. Perhaps I can do no better than to quote you the entire table of contents of the 44-page issue (number two) which I have in hand: "GADGETRY: The Cars of James Bond"; "GADGETRY: The Minox Spy Camera"; "AGENTS: Francis Gary Powers"; "BOOKS: Spies on the Shelf"; "WRITERS: Steven Jay Rubin"; "DEBRIEFING: Espionage News"; "WEAPONS: Beretta"; "CRYPTOGRAPHY: Basic Word Codes." What more can I say?

MIKE COOK'S MONTHLY MURDERS

Several of our people have just had books published, and I am delighted to be able to tout them here. First, there's Mike Cook's *Monthly Murders: A Checklist and Chronological Listing of Fiction in the Digest-Size Mystery Magazines in the United States and England* (Greenwood Press [88 Post Road West, Westport, CT 06881], 1982, 1147 pp., $49.95). What we have here in this huge and handsomely bound volume is a listing of the contents of (virtually) every issue of (virtually) every American or British digest-sized magazine between 1941, when *Ellery Queen's Mystery Magazine* began its career as the first of the popular digest-sized mystery magazines, and the end of 1980. God knows how many separate stories appear in the 763 pages that make up the table of contents listings--Mike does not say, and I'll be damned if I'll count them--but I did count the number of magazine titles that are indexed: 110. The last third of the book is an alphabetical index by author, and under each author entry appears an alphabetical listing of those of his stories which are cited in the first part of the book, keyed to show the name, volume, and number of the magazine in which each appeared.

How useful is this book? Well, I just wish I had had it when we were doing the Stout bibliography a few years back. I was chagrined to find in Mike's listings more than one or two magazine appearances that we had overlooked. I would call this an absolutely indispensable tool for any researcher in the field. No library should be without it, nor should any fan who can afford to part with half a hundred bucks. Perhaps, after I've used it a couple of years, I'll be able to come up with a fair collection of complaints, but after my so-far brief acquaintance about the only cavil I have (except for wishing that Mike had cited inclusive page numbers for each article) is that the two-letter code used to identify the magazines in the author index is not incorporated into the

running heads. As a result one cannot, after looking up a
story in the author index, simply turn immediately to the main
entry; instead, one must go back to the front of the book
(where the codes are identified in an alphabetical listing of
the magazines indexed), determine the magazine title to which
the code refers, and then find the appropriate magazine and,
finally, the main entry. Since the main body of the book,
like the index, is alphabetical, it would have simplified
matters greatly if the two-letter code had been incorporated
into the running heads. It's a little thing, sure, but I
couldn't let Mike get by without complaining about something.

BOB SAMPSON'S NIGHT MASTER

Unfortunately, there's no way I can let Bob Sampson get by
without complaining about a great deal. This is doubly unfor-
tunate, actually, since most of the things about which I shall
complain are not his fault. As TMF readers know, Bob is a
highly knowledgeable and entertaining writer, as fine a hand
at turning a phrase as we have in our midst. As he imparts
information to us he also brings smiles to our lips and laugh-
ter from our mouths. If he can do that in the short articles
which appear in these pages, imagine what he could do in a
book-length treatment of one ·of the pulps about which he is
so unquestionably an expert. Now keep that thought in your
mind as I plod onward.

Robert Sampson. *The Night Master.* Pulp Press (1545 Ox-
ford Drive, Oak Forest, IL 60452), 1982, 216 pp., illustrated,
$14.95.

Physically, it's an extremely handsome book. The book itself is sewn and bound in black leatherette. It contains
three full-page illustrations by the wonderfully skillful
Frank Hamilton plus twelve additional pages of illustrations
from *The Shadow Magazine* itself (including twenty-four covers,
reproduced four to a page). Slipped inside the front cover of
the copy I have is another Hamilton illustration, loose this
time, signed by both Sampson and Hamilton. The whole lovely
package is wrapped in a dust jacket graced by yet another fine
piece of Frank Hamilton's art.

As you will already have guessed, *The Night Master* is Bob
Sampson's history of The Shadow in his various manifestations
--the character, the radio series, the magazine. There are
some fictional characters who have a higher recognition factor
than The Shadow, but there aren't many. Despite this well-
nigh universal awareness, I dare say that only a tiny fraction
of the populace--even of so informed a group as the readership
of TMF--has extensive first-hand knowledge of "The Night Master." The last issue of *The Shadow Magazine* appeared thirty-
three years ago, and there have been few things in human history more ephemeral than pulp magazines, which is a large part
of the reason they are so damned expensive nowadays. Even
were that not so--even if they were as plentiful in today's
used book shops as paperback editions of *The Godfather*--it is
questionable that all that many modern readers would devote
much of their time to reading through the prose that Walter
Gibson ground out at the rate of more than a million words a
year for over a decade. Tastes change, and there's so very
much reading material available which is more attuned to our
(Continued on page 10)

The Policeman: A Victorian Novel

By E. F. Bleiler

In the history of British police and detective systems, so much emphasis is placed on the policing of London (both the City and the Metropolis) that one tends to forget that other areas of Great Britain had problems with both crime and police.

Such a place, in the early nineteenth century, was Liverpool, which, before industrialization had set in heavily, was a gigantic staging area, partly for emigrants heading for the United States or the colonies, partly for Irish and Scottish immigrants looking for work in more prosperous England. Liverpool was a crime center for transients, yet its new commercial prosperity also aroused feelings of local chauvinism. Both aspects of Liverpool emerge in the anonymous *Life, Adventures, and Opinions of a Liverpool Policeman and His Contemporaries* (printed by E. Matthews, published by Messrs. Booker and Co. and Mr. Barnes, Liverpool, 1841, 725 pp., with eighteen copperplates). This book is also known by its short title, *The Policeman*, which appears on the spine and the running heads.

A long, amorphous novel, *The Policeman* begins in a Liverpool coffee room as two young men about town strike up a conversation with two policemen, who, surprisingly enough, are gentlemen as well as servants of Her Majesty. The superior officer, Inspector George Mugginson (later sometimes spelled Muggynson), is induced to talk of his past history.

It soon becomes obvious, though, that Mugginson himself is of no great interest except as a narrator. His story focuses on Joseph Villanose Floss, a plausible, daring scoundrel whose name and exploits are probably deliberately suggestive of *The Memoirs of James Hardy Vaux* (1819), a well-known pseudofactual crime autobiography.

In the words of *Hue and Cry*, as read in the dialect of a fellow criminal, Floss is:

Height, five feetsh nine, slender though of powerful shimeter [meaning?], aqualine [*sic*] noshe, light hair, dark piercing eyst, small feet, and a remarkable spring in his walk, and about twenty-six years of agish, of great suavity of mannersh, and preposhing [prepossessing], and engaging.

Floss's exploits are told chiefly in two long sections, the reminiscences of Mugginson in the first part of the novel, and a very long letter that Floss later sends to Mugginson from

Australia.

Floss's career begins when he accepts Mugginson as an
assistant in a crooked business scheme. Although Floss poses
as a vender of porter, he is really engaged in swindling and
passing bad bills. When he is discovered, he first hides out
in Liverpool in the guise of a French traveler, and then, with
Mugginson, takes passage to Dublin. They are followed to Dublin by Sharpwrit, their crooked attorney, who hopes to collect
a reward of one hundred pounds that is offered for Floss, and
by O'Mazem, an Irish bounty hunter. But Floss is more than a
match for them; he contrives to have O'Mazem arrest Sharpwrit
and then politely blackmails O'Mazem for the mistake.

Things get too hot for Floss and Mugginson in Ireland, and
to hide out for a time they enlist in Her Majesty's Horse
Dragoons. Floss cannot resist loot and robs his fellow sol-
diers, shifting the blame on to an enemy by planting evidence.
But this time Floss is found out and he is forced to run for
his life.

Mugginson has by now come to realize that Floss's mode of
life is too deep for him, and, as sometimes happens with semi-
picaros, he decides to reform. Like Tom Richmond in *Richmond:
Scenes in the Life of a Bow Street Runner* (1827), he joins the
police force:

> Finding how other literary gentlemen had sprung up in the police,
> though, like me, perhaps they had embraced that profession as a
> *dernier resort*, I was resolved to emulate so glorious an example
> ... and became a progressive constable, at eighteen shillings a
> week.

He finds a person who will stand bond for him so that he can
draw a uniform, is assigned to a beat in Liverpool, and thereafter assumes the duties of a foot patrol. Households give
him small gifts and bribes for services, but he is pressured
to share these rewards with his old acquaintance O'Mazem, who
has turned up as his superior officer.

At this point in the exposition Muggins drops out of the
novel, in effect, except for brief later appearances, and
other matters serve as fillers. The author now offers sentiment, adventure, humor, personality grotesques, often expressed
in a range of dialects--Irish, North Country, Midlands, Scottish, Yiddish, Cockney, and perhaps others that I do not recognize.

Floss's second group of exploits, starting about 150 pages
later, is described in a long letter that Floss sends Mugginson from Australia.

After deserting from the army, Floss circulates openly in
criminal circles, despite a reward of £500 on his head. While
traveling, he spots two likely flats (suckers), Potman and Sir
Patrick MacCaisey, and determines to use their wealth to pay
for passage to Australia, where he expects to find opportunity
for his talents. He watches them being twelved by smiths
(cheated by cardsharps) in a gambling den, and in a bold play
he manages to cut in on the trick, taking the part of the
pigeons (suckers). This episode introduces Floss's most note-
worthy adventure.

Floss notes that the sharps have an accomplice in the person of a seemingly respectable old man, and he is thus prepared
when the old man sneaks away with the gambling stakes. Floss's

companion and servant follows the old man, and Floss visits
him the next day. He reveals his identity and demands satis-
faction--part of the plunder. The old man, Flammer, makes a
counter offer. He suggests that Floss take up counterfeiting
in Australia, and he is willing to introduce him to the finest
maker of coining dies in England. This man, Phiptip, is the
despair of the mints of Europe, so remarkable is his work, yet
he is so canny that he has never been caught.

Floss visits Phiptip and engages him to make a die for
coining sovereigns. While he is in Phiptip's apartments, the
place is raided by Bow Street runners, who vainly search for
evidence. They are not successful, for Phiptim has his wares
hidden in a secret drawer.

When Floss leaves, he is accosted by the runners, with
whom he strikes a bargain. He agrees to betray Phiptip in
exchange for immunity and Ł2,000. The runners accept, as does
the government.

Floss and his servant return to Phiptip, having arranged
for the runners to break in when the servant makes a signal in
front of the window. Everything seems to go according to plan,
but when the runners seize Phiptip they discover that once
again he has been too clever for them. Suspicious at the servant's actions, he had substituted for the coin die a die
suitable for manufacturing coat buttons--and sent the incriminating piece away by carrier pigeon. Floss, as a result of
this fiasco, does not get the reward and has made a powerful
enemy in Phiptip. He has also discredited himself with the
criminal class by turning nark. But his reputation for sav-
agery and violence is such that he is not molested.

Floss now falls back on a scheme to get money from the
flats Potman and Sir Patrick. He builds up a quarrel that has
arisen between the two men and contributes to the ensuing duel
a set of magician's pistols: if one squeezes the trigger while
loading the gun, the bullet drops out; if the bullet is re-
tained in the pistol, the gun fires at a peculiar, predictable
angle. Before the duel Floss manages to squeeze the bullet
out of Sir Patrick's gun so that he is defenseless, and he ad-
vises Potman to shoot in such a fashion (though Potman thinks
he will miss) that Sir Patrick is killed. Potman breaks down
when he sees that he has killed his friend, and Floss hastens
him away. Despite a boat chase by the police, they leave
Liverpool for Australia.

In Australia, Floss soon becomes head of a gang of bushrangers and evolves another scheme. Among Her Majesty's guests
in Australia is the former attorney of a wealthy family who
knows the circumstances of a missing heir to a fortune. (A
large part of the previous development had been devoted to
this heir, Abel Poordevil.) Floss's agents in England are to
murder Abel, anf Floss will send a false claimant from Australia.

But retribution finally arrives. Phiptip, the diemaker,
sends word to his criminal friends in Australia about Floss's
treachery, and Potman learns how Floss manipulated the pistols
to cause the death of Sir Patrick. The bushrangers, angered
by Floss's working with the police and motivated by rewards
offered by Potman, disavow Floss, and he is hunted across the
land by native trackers with dingos. When he is captured, he
is crucified, and he dies on the cross. In a travesty of the
Crucifixion, two outlaws gamble beneath him as he hangs dying.

In an unsigned preface, the publishers state that *The Policeman* was written by a young Liverpool merchant of "high standing on 'Change,'" who, because of the death of a relative, departed for a "far distant clime," leaving the manuscript behind to the judgment of friends. For this reason, the publishers admit, the novel begins abruptly, without true introduction.

Whether this statement is true or just editorial persiflage we do not know, for there is no further information about the author of *The Policeman*. On the face of it, however, the publishers' statement seems improbable. One would expect an involved novel of a half-million words or more to be the work of a practiced hack, rather than of a busy young merchant who belonged to the Exchange.

As for *The Policeman* itself, it is fairly typical of subculture novels of the 1830's and 40's, which were extremely long meandering works without central themes or statements. Features common to such novels are a roughly biographical outline; a strong picaresque element; a closed universe of a dozen or two characters who appear over and over in various roles; a variety of story textures (criminal, sentimental, humorous, adventurous); grotesque characters; a wealth of local color; a lower middle class orientation; and formal chaos. Dickens worked in and out of this general pattern, though he was able to provide a control over his material that minor writers, like the author of *The Policeman,* lacked.

Within this range of "all things to all readers" a modern can select what is of interest to him. In this case, the adventures of Floss. Surprisingly enough, Floss's encounter with Phiptip the diemaker is fairly well handled, with a couple of good characterizations, reasonable dialogue, and some excellent detail.

The remainder of the novel, though, is probably not going to be pleasure reading for a modern, although a student of historical slang will find in it quite a few locutions not in Partridge.

(Continued from page 6) present tastes that even the very best of the pulps are now neglected by readers, if not by collectors.

A paucity of both time and money (combined with a general disinclination to burden myself with yet another enthusiasm) has kept me from becoming a pulp collector and reader, but I do have an interest in the pulps. (I don't think there's any great contradiction there: I also have an interest in Antarctic exploration, but it hasn't led me to volunteer for any South Polar expeditions.) And that is precisely why Bob Sampson is such a treasure. Bob *has* read them--hell, he's *studied* them--and he has the talent to make his love and enthusiasm for the pulps come alive in those of us who never have. Bob enables us to experience the pulps vicariously, without investing tremendous amounts of time and money in them. For some of us, this vicarious experience is enough. For others, Bob Sampson may well be a viral infection; some may be bitten by the same bug that has Bob firmly in its jaws, and they may hare off into the countryside, slavering for the chance to lay their twitching hands on a stack of yellowing pages wrapped in a lurid cover depicting menacing villains, toothsome maidens, and cloaked avengers.

(Continued on page 15)

Gide's "Vatican Cellars"
The Popular Detective Novel Parodied

By Pierre L. Horn

In addition to his fine novels, plays, and prose poetry,
André Gide, an avid reader of detective novels,[1] also wrote
such works as *The Immoralist* (1902) and *Isabelle* (1911), which
used devices of the police genre.[2] It is in *The Vatican Cellars* (1914), however, that he both employs and satarizes many
of the techniques of this popular literature. When he creates
the plot of this *sotie*, it is from an old newspaper article[3]
that he draws his inspiration. Taking for a subject the false
imprisonment of Leo XIII by the freemasons in the Castle of
St. Angelo in Rome, Gide uses it to present characters who
seem to come directly from the French popular novel.

Criminals, organized in a vast international conspiracy
with the evocative name of "Millipede," take advantage of the
naive credulity of rich devout women to wheedle out of them
large sums of cash in order to pay for the hostage pope's ran-
som. They "demand two hundred thousand francs.... A hundred
and forty of the two hundred thousand have been subscribed
already.... The Duchesse de Lectoure has ... promised ...
fifty; there remain sixty to be found,"[4] which the Countess de
Saint-Prix remits under the threat of a long stay in purgatory.
The crooks have accomplices everywhere, in banks, trains ("the
waiter and the widow and the little girl are all in it too"
[p. 220]), hotels, post offices ("As was to be expected, the
Millipede had confederates there too.... Protos ... had no
difficulty in getting an obliging employee to hand him over a
letter of Arnica's" [p. 136]). The gang has branches in numerous cities in France, as well as in Italy. Honest men, the
"crustacés" (fossilized) par excellence, falsely believing
themselves to have free will in this sham world governed by

---

[1] See André Gide, *Journal* (Paris: "Bibliothèque de la Pléiade," Galli-
mard, 1951 and 1954), I: 1136-37, II: 124, 213.

[2] A discussion of these can be found in Pierre L. Horn, *"Isabelle*: A
Detective Novel by André Gide," *Romance Notes* 18 (1977): 1-8.

[3] Abbot Joseph Waé, *Compte rendu de la Délivrance de Sa Sainteté Léon
XIII, emprisonné dans les cachots du Vatican de Pâques 1892 à Pâques 1893*
(Saint-Malo: Y. Billois, 1893).

[4] André Gide, *The Vatican Cellars*, translated by Dorothy Bussy (London:
Penguin Books, 1959), p. 94. Hereafter, all quotations are from this
translation and are cited in parentheses within the text.

the forces of evil, are in fact spied upon, tricked, flouted, guided by the members of this occult brotherhood: "You're to keep your client company in his walks.... Don't lose sight of him" (p. 135).

Protos, symbolically named, is the uncontested and omnipotent leader of this grandiose swindling enterprise. Of the same family as Vautrin, Fantômas, Zigomar, and Arsène Lupin, he has, like them, the gift of being whom he wants: "His features were extraordinarily illuminating ... and could express anything and everything" (pp. 79-80). Thus, he can appear disguised as a priest in front of Hadrian's Mausoleum ("from the face alone one would have recognized a priest, and from that peculiarly respectable something which distinguished him --a French priest" [p. 137]), as a white-haired and young-faced canon at Mme. de Saint-Prix's, as a simple Calabrese peasant in the Rome-Naples express ("in his new aspect, with his open shirt, his brown breeches, his sandals, laced over his blue stockings, his short pipe and his tan-colored hat with its small flat brim, it must be admitted that he looked far more like a regular Abruzzi brigand than like a *curé*" [p. 144]). He shows up, under the wonderful name of Defouque- blize, as a professor of comparative criminology at the Bor- deaux School of Law, in the dining-car of the Naples-Rome train. He is so well disguised that even his former classmate does not recognize him: "You mustn't desert an old friend like this, Mr. Lafcadio What-the-deuceki" (p. 215). Despite all his disguises, however, Protos can be uncovered easily by the reader from a sentence he utters at each delay: "For the mat- ter of that!"

Of course, André Gide does not limit himself only to the apparent devices of the detective novel, such as gangs of thieves and the crafty disguises of a modern Proteus. He especially wants to develop the ethic he had already sketched out in *Marshlands* and *Prometheus Misbound* through the concept of the *gratuitous act*. He will, therefore, use one of the most important conventionalisms of the police story, the per- fect crime.

The most famous of Gidean gratuitous actors is young Laf- cadio. However, although he seeks to commit only a motiveless crime by killing Amédée Fleurissoire, he is actually questing for the perfect crime:

> Who would see?... There,... under my hand, this double fastening, which I can easily undo; the door would suddenly give way and he would topple out; the slightest push would do it; he would fall into the darkness like a stone; one wouldn't even hear a scream. ... And off tomorrow to the east!... Who would know?... What a puzzle for the police! (p. 184).

But Gide does not want to help out this murderer, and this is why he purposely places clues here and there which any good policeman could easily find. Two of these clues are partic- ularly conspicuous by their recurring appearance through the book: the cuff-links and the beaver hat. Let us look at each one.

The cuff-links, of an especially bad taste, a gift from Lafcadio to Carola, have in turn been given by her to Fleuris- soire and noticed by the all-seeing Protos. Now that Gide has shown the actual presence of these cuff-links on Amédée, he

surreptitiously puts one in the train compartment: "He [Fleur-
issoire] flung his right [cuff-link] well behind him and over
Lafcadio's head, sending his second cuff-link ... spinning to
the other end of the carriage, where it rolled underneath the
seat" (p. 185), and slyly leaves the other on the cuff. The
police immediately note the comparison, and Carola too has
recognized the victim by the newspapers' description of these
horrible cuff-links. Lafcadio will admit his mistake when he
tries to pocket the incriminating evidence:

> With a sweep of his hand, Lafcadio wipes his plate and brushes the
> horrid trinket onto the table-cloth,... seizes the link, slips it
> into his waistcoat pocket.... Why did he take a sleeve-link which
> doesn't belong to him? What an admission is implied by this in-
> stinctive and absurd action--what a recognition! How he has given
> himself away to the people ... who are watching him.... He has
> walked straight into their booby trap like a fool (pp. 211-12).

The second clue, the beaver hat, represents another mistake on Lafcadio's part. In his fatal fall Amédée grabbed the
murderer's hat, and, despite the owner's precaution of cutting
out his initials, the hat-maker's label still remains inside.
A few days later, however, he reads in the paper: "His left
hand was found still clutching a soft felt hat.... The maker's
name has been carefully removed from the lining, out of which
a piece of leather has been cut to the size and shape of a
laurel leaf" (pp. 197-98). Lafcadio understands at once that
"his crime had been tampered with; someone had touched it up;
had cut the piece out of the lining" (p. 198). This "someone"
who had the kindness (and the insolence) to correct Lafcadio's
mistakes is none other than Protos. Not only does Protos
scold him for having picked up the cuff-link from the plate
but also for having worn such an elegant hat on the day of the
crime: "To wear a hat of that kind on one's head when one's
out on the job!... With the hatter's address in the lining
too! Why! you'd have been collared before the week was out."
(p. 216).
Who, then, is this Lafcadio Wluiki? We can see that he
has many ties with French popular heroes, and with Arsène
Lupin in particular. Both, though illegitimate, are of aristocratic blood, both have been abandoned by their fathers at a
very early age. Lafcadio is a complex synthesis of the gentle-
man and the scoundrel and can just as easily strangle an old
woman as help her with her packages. Like Lupin, he is a
"bizarre compound of intelligence and perversion, of immorality
and generosity."[5] As such, he risks his life saving children
from a burning house while he kills an unknown individual almost for a game. As a matter of fact, he knows very well that
he is a constant danger for society, from which he feels completely alienated: "If I were the Government, I should lock
myself up" (p. 178). He has indeed the primitive and murder-
ous instinct of the barbarian under the refinement and polish
of the man of the world, and therefore he can be considered as
the only "subtil" (sly one) of the novel.[6]

[5] Maurice Leblanc, *Arsène Lupin, gentleman-cambrioleur* in *Les Adventures
d'Arsène Lupin* (Paris: Hachette/Gillimard, 1960), I:330.

[6] For a study of this theme, see Pierre L. Horn, "On a Whitman Quotation

Dramatic turns of events are not absent either from the narrative, from the pope's kidnapping by followers of the French Lodge to the revealing of Lafcadio's noble ancestry, from Anthime Armand-Dubois's miraculous cure to his no less miraculous relapse. However, it is in the last part of the work that we find most of the plot-twists and surprises: the incomprehensible theft of Lafcadio's suitcase ("when [he] got back to his compartment, his portmanteau was gone!... [It] was calmly proceeding on its way in company of a strapping fellow who was carrying it off at a leisurely walk" [p. 188]); the sudden appearance of the cuff-link ("there, right in front of him, plain to his sight in the very middle of his plate, fallen from God knows where, frightful and unmistakable among a thousand there lies Carola's sleeve-link" [p. 211]); the unexpected and mistaken arrest of Fleurissoire's murderer.

Whereas Gide's other novels are peopled with flesh-and-blood characters, *The Vatican Cellars* is filled with puppets, of which the author pulls the strings and which he does not take very seriously. For instance, he enjoys addressing his young hero: "Lafcadio, my friend, here you require the pen of a newspaper reporter--mine abandons you! My readers must not expect me to relate the incoherent comments of the onlookers, the broken exclamations, the ...' (p. 58); "Lafcadio, my friend, you are verging on the commonplace. If you are going to fall in love, do not count on my pen to paint the disturbance of your heart" (p. 69).

Amédée Fleurissoire is the special butt of André Gide's irony. Gone to Rome to deliver the pope, as the twelfth-century Crusaders went to the Holy Land to deliver Christ's tomb, he becomes the actor and victim of the quest he has undertaken. All the laughable adventures happen to him during his pilgrimage. In Marseilles he is bitten by bedbugs which, declares Gide, have "peculiar manners and customs; they wait till the candle is out, and then, as soon as it is dark, sally forth--not at random; they make straight for the neck, the place of their predilection; sometimes they select the wrists; a few rare ones prefer the ankles" (p. 120). In Toulon, second stop, "it was fleas.... He felt them creeping up and down his legs, tickling the small of his back, inoculating him with fever" (p. 122). In Genoa, third stop, a small mosquito stings him "on the left side of his nose,... on his wrist. Then right against his ear there sounded the mocking of an impertinent buzzing.... Horror! He had shut the enemy up within the citadel!" (p. 125). The grotesque interludes have no relation to the mission that Fleurissoire has given himself, or to the rest of the story, and thus satirize the adventure novel from Chrétien de Troyes to Ponson du Terrail.

Gide also parodies the detective *roman-feuilleton* by exaggerating the methods of the genre. Lafcadio, who is suspicious of everyone, protects his belongings by rather odd means: "He directed his eyes towards the drawer, in opening which Julius had unwittingly destroyed a minute and almost invisible seal of soft wax" (p. 52). Fleurissoire, fortunately warned by Protos, feels constantly watched and spied upon: "I turned round a dozen times to make sure that I wasn't being followed. ... I see nothing but spies everywhere.... I see something disquieting in the appearance of everyone I pass in the street.

It alarms me if they look at me, and if they don't look at me, they seem as if they were pretending not to see me" (p. 144). Finally, Gide has had the excellent idea of ending his book with two questions, also after the manner of popular novel writers: "He [Lafacadio] listens ... to the vague rumor of the town as it begins to shake off its torpor.... What! Is he going to renounce life?... Does he still think of giving himself up?" (p. 237). For the resemblance to be even more noticeable, all that is missing is the three famous words that conclude every installment: *To be continued....*

Not only did Gide want to accord detective literature an important place, but he wanted also to incorporate its narrative techniques in the modern novel, from Simenon to Robbe-Grillet. François Mauriac's remark concerning *The Vatican Cellars* summarizes very well the interest of the novel: "André Gide wagered himself to write a police novel which would have merit through its invention and plot. He told himself that by lending life and truculence to the characters of his imbroglio he would thrust into high literature the somewhat discredited genre of the dime novel."[7] André Gide has indeed succeeded.

---

[7] **François Mauriac,** *Les Cahiers de la Quinzaine,* 15 May 1914, p. 27.

(Continued from page 10)
Bob Sampson's *Night Master* is a fine study, but it can be a real pain to read. Not because of Bob's writing, which, though it could use tightening up here and there (as whose could not?), is delightful as you would expect; but because of the embarrassingly amateurish way in which the book has been assembled. To begin with, the layout of the book defies virtually every book-production convention known to man. The instances are far too many to list, but they begin with the half-title page, which is numbered "1" instead of "i" (of course, the number "1" does not actually appear, but it is obvious from subsequent pagination that if it did it would be an arabic rather than a roman numeral). Then, when you get to the table of contents (on page "6" for God's sake!), you discover another peculiarity: the book is divided into four chapters of almost comically varying lengths. The first is 95 pages, the second 23, the third 23, and the fourth is eight. Clearly, when one chapter is very nearly twice as long as all the other chapters put together, something is amiss. This could easily have been alleviated by dividing the one long chapter into several smaller ones, and even if this did not occur to Bob (writers, like other folks, sometimes can't see the forest for the trees), it certainly should have occurred to his publisher.

Getting into the text itself, the first thing one is struck by is the way the type is used. I'm not one of those birds who can identify any typeface on earth at twenty paces on a moonless night, and I wouldn't want to argue the merits of Caslon over Bruce even if I could tell the difference. I'm not, therefore, complaining about the font selected; in fact, it's very pleasing. What I am referring to is much more basic. There is a convention in publishing that book titles (among other things) be given in italics. In typescripts, that convention is satisfied by underlining the words in question, and a more relaxed and easier alternative (albeit one with some
(Continued on page 18)

Some Recent Hybrids

By George Kelley

Randall Garrett. *Lord Darcy Investigates*. Ace, 1981.
James Herbert. *The Jonah*. Signet, 1981.
E.C. Tubb. *The Terridae (Dumarest of Terra #25)*, DAW, 1981.
Mike McQuay. *Mathew Swain: Hot Time in Old Town*. Bantam,
1981. *Mathew Swain: When Trouble Beckons*. Bantam, 1981.

Mixing genres is a risky enterprise, and these works blend
mystery and science fiction/fantasy with mixed results.
Randall Garrett has been writing about Lord Darcy, Chief
Investigator for the Duke of Normandy, since 1964. Lord Darcy
investigates impossible crimes but the twist is the setting of
the stories: an alternate world where magic works while science
is looked upon with suspicion. The "magic" is actually psi
powers developed by the Laws of Magic. The semi-medieval,
twentieth-century civilization Garrett develops is convincing
both for the primitive science the aristocratic society scorns
and for the sophisticated magic most characters possess.
The interesting point here is that Lord Darcy possesses no
psi powers--for that he relies on his sorcerous assistant,
Sean O'Lochlainn. Instead, Lord Darcy uses induction and de-
duction to pull off amazing Sherlockian solutions to the in-
credible puzzles Garrett presents him with.
Lord Darcy Investigates is a collection of four novelettes:
"A Matter of Gravity," "The Ipswich Phial," "The Sixteen Keys,"
and "The Napoli Express." In "A Matter of Gravity," Lord Darcy
solves a locked-room murder with a double twist ending. In
"The Ipswich Phial," Lord Darcy becomes involved in an espionage mission featuring a beautiful Polish spy, a murdered British agent, and a missing secret weapon. This is the best
story in the volume. "The Sixteen Keys" presents the puzzle
of a dead man in a house with sixteen locked doors. And "The
Napoli Express" has more deception than Agatha Christie's *Murder on the Orient Express*. I highly recommend *Lord Darcy In-
vestigates* and the other Lord Darcy volumes, *Too Many Magicians*
(Doubleday, 1967; Ace 1981), a novel, and *Murder and Magic*
(Ace, 1979, 1981), a collection of four more novelettes.
James Herbert has established himself as one of the lead-
ing British horror novelists with chillers like *The Rats*, *The
Fog*, *Survivor*, *Fluke*, *Lair*, *The Spear*, and *The Dark*.
His latest novel, *The Jonah*, features Undercover policeman
Jim Kelso as a jinxed man, a jonah no one will work with.
Through a series of flashbacks, Herbert shows Kelso's early

16

life in England--his abandonment at birth, the horror of the
orphanage in post-WW II Britain. Even then, death struck
those around Kelso--when bullies chase him into an abandoned
house, a savage death befalls them. Later, Kelso finds his
step-father mysteriously dead, and a few years after that the
woman he lives with dies in horrible circumstances.

When Kelso begins his career with the police, misfortune
seems to strike those colleagues who work with him. Eventually,
because no one will work with him, Kelso is assigned to undercover assignments where he can work alone. Even so, whenever
a big bust comes down, the police involved with Kelso are
killed or injured.

As a last resort, Kelso is teamed with a woman undercover
agent, Ellie Shepherd. Together, they are supposed to break
up a drug ring operating around a NATO base where a pilot recently crashed into the sea while taking drugs on a mission.

Kelso stubbornly resists a romantic involvement with Ellie
and tries to discourage her from working with him on the
assignment before his jinx strikes her.

Although one of the pushers is murdered and an attempt is
made on their lives, Kelso and Ellie get closer and closer to
the secret of the drug ring. There's a solid presentation of
police procedure in all of this, but all the while Herbert
also generates a mood of rising terror through the use of his
flashbacks.

The final climactic scene is chilling but lacks the impact
of Herbert's classics, *The Spear* and *The Dark*. Nevertheless,
for a few hours of suspenseful reading, *The Jonah* will do.

The Terridae is the latest volume in E.C. Tubb's Dumarest
Saga. Dumarest is a traveller of the far future. He's looking for his home planet, Earth. The catch is, nobody knows
where it is or even if it exists. Dumarest knows it exists,
because he left the bleak planet as a young boy by stowing
away on a starship. As the ship went deeper and deeper into
the galaxy, Dumarest lost his way. Now he's trying to find
his way back home. Unfortunately, a few volumes ago Dumarest
had the bad luck of running afoul of the Cyclan, an organization of modified humans seeking to dominate the galaxy. Dumarest stole the secret of the affinity twin, which allows the
possessor to control the mind of another, and the Cyclan has
been chasing him around the galaxy ever since to relieve him
of the secret. Dumarest escapes time and again through the
use of luck and random movement.

In the present adventure, Dumarest discovers a religious
group, the Terridae, whose sole goal is to find Earth. Dumarest must discover their secret before the Cyclan discovers
him. As space opera, the Dumarest Saga is uneven. Several of
the adventures are top-notch--*Toyman*, *Veruchia*, and *Eloise*--
while others are weak--*Technos*, *Jondelle*, and *The Terridae*.
In fact, Tubb leaves *The Terridae* open for a quick sequel. One
hopes it will be a bit more innovative and better developed
than the fragmented *Terridae*. However, Dumarest's quest for
Earth, with its slow, painful gathering of clues as to Earth's
location in book after book, has the attractive power of all
good serials and keeps fans reading even the mediocre novels
in the series.

Mike McQuay's transfer of the clichés of the private eye
novel into the twenty-first century can only be considered a
dumb joke. McQuay--who dedicates the Mathew Swain series to

Raymond Chandler--seems only to write in bad clichés. Here's
the opening paragraph of the first book in the series, *Hot
Time in Old Town:*

> Sometimes, when the wind blows just right and the hot summer
> rain steams the streets like the last foul breath of a concrete
> dragon, the smell of death rolls down from Old Town and hangs
> over the living like a hammer over an anvil--waiting. There's
> life in death, I suppose; the knowledge of the rind makes the
> taste of the melon sweeter. But then, I suppose a lot of things.
> That's why I make my living solving other people's problems.

The purple prose, the introspective manner, the philosophical
attitude are elements Chandler managed to avoid, while lesser
pulp writers turned Chandler's subtle approach into heavy-
handed, leadened similes and cardboard characters.
    McQuay's Mathew Swain is a violent, tough-talking private
eye, closer to Mickey Spillane's killing machine, Mike Hammer,
than to Chandler's thinking-man's detective, Philip Marlowe.
There's little detection here; Swain mostly gets shot at,
attacked, and insulted by the police. The future Swain in-
habits is a hostile environment similar to John Brunner's
Jagged Orbit, the ultimate in urban violence. The police are
mercenaries working for the highest bidder; the rich live in
armored palaces; the poor kill each other to survive.
    In *Hot Time in Old Town* Swain is hired by a rich old man
to find out who murdered his son--reminiscent of Chandler's
Big Sleep. Swain bumbles about through a clanking plot until
clues lead him to Old Town, a mutant enclave created by the
meltdown of a nuclear powerplant. Swain finds the solution,
which is taken from another Chandler novel, *The Long Goodbye.*
Most of the book is poorly written, but the scenes of Old
Town are compelling.
    When Trouble Beckons, the sequel to *Hot Time in Old Town,*
is a shoddy piece of work. Swain leaves Earth for the Moon to
help investigate a murder. There, with the help of a woman
cabbie, he takes on the vicious gang that runs the company
town. The plot swings wildly from one improbability to the
next with McQuay throwing in some violence whenever the plot
starts to falter from all the unlikely situations Swain finds
himself in. This is comic-book writing in paperback form.
    Read *Lord Darcy Investigates,* and take your chances on
the rest.

(Continued from page 15) drawbacks) is typing titles in full
caps, THUSLY. Underlining and full capitalization are, however, only *substitutes* to be used only when italic fonts are
not available. It is, therefore, quite jarring to find that
the book and magazine titles in *The Night Master* are given in
full caps rather than italics. (I should say, "are *usually*
given," since someone slipped up in the Acknowledgements sec-
tion and acutally used italics correctly in a couple of places.)
It is not that an italic font was not available, since italics
are used throughout to highlight certain words--which incidentally, would have been better highlighted by putting *them*
in full caps.
    As you read along, other screw-ups leap from the pages to
grab your eyeballs. On at least two occasions, whoever pasted
(Continued on page 20)

Spy Series Characters in Hardback Part XI

By Barry Van Tilburg

DOSSIER #56: Gunston Cotton.
CREATED BY: Rupert Grayson.
OCCUPATION: Agent for the British Foreign Office.
ASSOCIATES: His boss, X; his fellow agents, "Coffin" Prescott
and Charles Cazelton; his wife, Tony.
WEAPONS: Pistols.
OTHER COMMENTS: Cotton is a British agent, but he often runs
into espionage plots on his own when he is not on assign-
ment. He was an air ace during World War II; after an
accident, he quit the flying game and went into espionage.
Gun Cotton (Newnes, 1934).
Gun Cotton--Secret Agent (Grayson, 1934; published as *Secret
Agent in Africa* by Dutton, 1939).
Death Rides the Forest (Grayson, 1934; Dutton, 1938).
Gun Cotton--Adventurer (Grayson, 1935; Dutton, 1937).
Escape with Gun Cotton (Grayson, 1935).
Gun Cotton Goes to Russia (Grayson, 1936).
Gun Cotton--Outside the Law (Grayson, 1936).
Gun Cotton in Hollywood (Grayson, 1937).
Gun Cotton--Ace High (Grayson, 1937).
Gun Cotton--Adventure Nine (Grayson, 1937).
Gun Cotton in Mexico (Grayson, 1937).
Gun Cotton at Blind Man's Hood (Grayson, 1938).
Gun Cotton--Secret Airman (Grayson, 1939).
Gun Cotton--Murder at the Bank (Grayson, 1939).

DOSSIER #57: Richard Raven.
CREATED BY: John Griffin.
OCCUPATION: Adventurer and free-lance counter-espionage agent.
ASSOCIATES: Alan Drive, his sometimes boss.
WEAPONS: Anything handy.
OTHER COMMENTS: The series is extremely violent. In *St. Cath-
erine's Wheel* the bad guy keeps various pieces of bodies
alive for some outrageous purpose which at first is unknown.
In *The Camelot Conundrum* Raven cuts off various portions
of bad guy's bodies with a sword.
The Midas Operation (Hale, 1976).
Standing into Danger (Hale, 1976).
Circle of Darkness (Hale, 1977).
Seeds of Destruction (Hale, 1977).
Anarchist's Moon (Hale, 1977).
Ring of Kerry (Hale, 1978).

St. Catherine's Wheel (Hale, 1978).
The Antarctic Convergence (Hale, 1979).
The Florentine Madonna (Hale, 1979).
The Camelot Conundrum (Hale, 1980).
A Flame from Persepolis (Hale, 1981).

DOSSIER #58: Roger Fleming.
CREATED BY: Simon Harvester (Henry St. John Clair Rumbold-
    Gibbs).
OCCUPATION: Agent for British Intelligence.
ASSOCIATES: Mark Blunden, an amateur that Fleming keeps run-
    ning into overseas. Three of the books are referred to as
    Mark Blunden adventures but still retain the running series
    character of Fleming. Renfrew, an agent partner of R.F.
WEAPONS: Revolvers.
OTHER COMMENTS: The books are violent but not overly so. In
    Maybe a Trumpet Fleming is looking for a Nazi agent con-
    cealed in a traveling circus. The character of Fleming is
    not very strong, which may be why Harvester wasn't included
    in *Twentieth Century Crime and Mystery Writers*.
Let Them Prey (Rich & Cowan, 1942).
Epitaph for Lemmings (Rich & Cowan, 1943; MacMillan, 1944).
Maybe a Trumpet (Rich and Cowan, 1945).
A Breastplate for Aaron (Rich & Cowan, 1950).
Sheep May Safely Graze (Rich & Cowan, 1950).
Obols for Charon (Jarrolds, 1951).
The Vessel May Carry Explosives (Jarrolds, 1951).

DOSSIER #59: Claude Ravel.
CREATED BY: Bradford Jones.
OCCUPATION: Starts series as a security officer for the Brit-
    ish cabinet; later works for Interpol.
ASSOCIATES: Monique, his wife, who formerly worked for the
    Deuxieme Bureau; James Keene, head of Cabinet Security;
    Peter Calvert, Cabinet Security's electronics expert.
WEAPONS: Ravel is ruthless and extremely violent, which is
    often a problem. He is in constant hot water with his
    boss over his excessive use of violence; this condition
    leads to his freelancing for Interpol.
The Hamlet Problem (Robert Hale, 1962).
The Crooked Phoenix (Robert Hale, 1962).
Tiger from the Shadows (Robert Hale, 1963).
Private Vendetta (Robert Hale, 1964).
Death on a Pale Horse (Robert Hale, 1965).
The Embers of Hate (Robert Hale, 1966).
Den of Savage Men (Robert Hale, 1967).
The Deadly Trade (Robert Hale, 1967).
The Shadowless Men (Robert Hale, 1970).

(Continued from page 18) up the pages got the copy out of order. In one instance it is only a matter of a few paragraphs;
in the other, two tables, of a combined length of more than a
page, are incongruously interspersed into a sentence broken by
a colon. On page 122, we read: "And between lay three pages
of small type which summarized the militant thoughts mailed in
by League members--each identified by his personal code number. Thus:" And at that point, about a third of the way down
the page, someone pasted in a table on "Variations in magazine
(Continued on page 26)

Reel Murders

Movie Reviews by Walter Albert

My mother once told me that the first time she and my
father took me to the movies, at the tender age of three, I
ruined the film for them and everyone in the immediate vicinity
by my refusal to sit still. I slid from my seat to the floor,
escaped to the aisle, and ran wantonly about until I was re-
trieved by my father and held firmly on his lap for the rest
of the showing. The next time they took me to the movies, my
father put candy in his coat pockets and lured me into sub-
missive viewing by the constant stuffing of sweets into my
eager mouth. I'm not sure that this anecdote is literally
true, since my mother has always had a fondness for embroider-
ing the real to make it more palatable, but I have been a con-
firmed movie addict since before I have any conscious memory
of it. I have been told by people who get fed up with my in-
satiable appetite for film that my film-going is the perfect
demonstration of a saying of Will Rogers which, altered to fit
my dissolute character, is as follows: "I never saw a film I
didn't like." This is not true, since I passionately disliked
at least one film I have seen in the last five years, but I
have seen very few films that I did not enjoy intermittently.
I do not like sports, but *Knute Rockne* and *Dallas North Forty*
gave me great pleasure; a weekend in the country depresses me,
but I have seen *Trail of the Lonesome Pine* and *Shepherd of the
Hills* innumerable times and I breathe in the bracing, simulated
mountain air with delight and thrill to the tall trees against
the blue sky; I get sea-sick if I smell epsom salts, but I can
sit for hours watching maritime dramas like *The Sea Wolf* or
the various versions of the Titanic disaster; and, incapable
of doing anything other than keep afloat in shallow water, at
4:00 on Saturday afternoon I often dive with Johnny Weismuller
into the studio backlot pool to wrestle with rubber crocodiles.
And I won't go into my fascination with the watery sexual meta-
morphosis of the chimney-sweep in *The Water Babies*.
There are probably many reasons for my movie obsession
(apart from that conditioning in the balcony of the Rialto
Theater), but perhaps it is true--as a friend who has known me
for years claims--that I can indulge all of my fantasies totally divorced from the restrictions of a mundane world. Recently,
part of the roof collapsed during a showing at the last of the
downtown Pittsburgh movie palaces, but, two days after the
theater re-opened following what I took to be successful re-
pairs, I was sitting in my aisle seat on the left side, uncon-

cerned about another collapse, picking my way carefully through the horrors of a futuristic New York in John Carpenter's *Escape from N.Y.* and dodging the flying bodies in Chuck Norris's *Eye for an Eye*. And this from a wimp who used to go eight blocks out of the way to avoid meeting up with the particular bully who had it in for him that year in public school. Movies are truly the Great Therapist and the Great Teat.

Last night as I sat up until 2:00 a.m. engrossed in a showing of the 20th Century Fox version of *Jane Eyre* (Dir.: Robert Stevenson, 1944), I alternately cursed the frequent interruptions for the promotion of albums like *Motels & Memories* and local entrepreneurs like Mother's Pizza ("Just like you remember it, only it really wasn't ever *this* good!") and revelled in the superb Dickensian detail of the sequences at Linwood School dominated by Henry Daniell's marvellous portrayal of the sadistic religious fanatic, Broadhurst. I was moved by the moody, romantic sweep of the episodes at Rochester's estate, with the brilliant portrayal of mad Mrs. Rochester's husband by Orson Welles, supported by one of composer Bernard Herrmann's finest scores. The film is one of those meticulous re-creations of a literary classic that David Selznick, in particular, was gifted in bringing to life on the screen, but it has, at moments, something which such films often do not have: imaginative camera work which makes portions of the film seem as fresh as they did thirty-five years ago and confirms for me the rumors that Welles, coming to this project after *Citizen Kane* and the abortive *Magnificent Ambersons,* co-directed certain scenes. I thought I detected Wellesian touches in Jane's introduction to Rochester at the manor; in the handling of the brief scene with Agnes Moorehead at the beginning as the camera in a sardonic low-angle shot accented the self-satisfied cruelty of Jane's aunt and cousin; and in the exterior shots of the great house that squats malevolently at the film's center, with its battlements and moody lighting that inevitably remind the viewer of Kane's estate. You will get some idea of the quality of the team that was assembled for this film when I tell you that two of the script-writers were Aldous Huxley and John Houseman and that, in addition to Welles, Daniell, Moorehead, and Joan Fontaine (as Jane), there are splendid performances by a group of actors that can only serve to remind us of the talent that was still available to the major studios in the early forties: Elizabeth Taylor, Peggy Ann Garner, Margaret O'Brien, Sara Allgood, John Sutton (in an uncommonly fine portrayal of Broadhurst's sympathetic alter ego, Dr. Rivers), and other players whose names are less familiar but whose faces are indelibly imprinted on our memories of films of the period. I was struck by the beauty of a line delivered by Welles as he described Jane's first sight of Mrs. Rochester, "Look at Jane, all grave and silent at the mouth of Hell," and bothered by the jarring modernity of another line describing Mrs. Rochester after her fatal leap as she "lay smashed on the pavement." I was riveted by a shot of Moorehead looking like a grinning Medusa and by the long shot of the wedding ceremony with the ominous entrance of an unseen "Guest" glimpsed only at first as a shadow slipping by against a shaft of light suddenly striking a sacristy wall. And I was intrigued by the obvious attempt to introduce fairy-tale elements into the narrative, with the climax clearly using devices from "Beauty and the Beast" that could not have been accidental.

In short, I was overwhelmed by the intelligence, crafts-
manship, and beauty of this film and reminded that film history is filled with superb movies that are often only entries
in an edition of *Movies That May Be Seen as Interruptions of
Late-Night TV Commercials*.
My enjoyment of this mystery film (even if the murders are
mostly psychological) was much keener than my reaction to any
of last year's crop of movies with detective and mystery
motifs. I was disappointed in *True Confessions*, which, in
spite of some fine acting by Robert Duvall and Kenneth Mac-
Millan, was, I thought, undermined by the underplaying of
Robert DeNiro that had something of the quality of a still-
life (poses with hands folded in priestly piety against a
textured background) with none of the enlivening detail that
distinguishes the gifted rendering from the routine. It was
also, in spite of some attractive photography, not conceived
of by its director as a "moving picture" and was more like one
of those heavy-handed period pieces that used to pass for high
drama.
Films are too seldom written about as experiences in seeing. Film is as rich and varied a medium as print, but it is
something quite different, and I believe that it is improper
to fault a film based on a novel or story because it "repro-
duces" imperfectly the "source." Fiction may provide a subject, a narrative of sorts, a character, but in the best films
that source is only a pretext to record something which the
director or filmwriter may have seen rather than read.
I must confess that I find my most satisfying evenings at
the movies to be at showings of silent films with their visual
grammar that is still as innovative and fresh today as the
styles of certain prose writers who have either seized the
essence of their medium and time or transcended it. With this
true confession made, I should like to inaugurate this column
with selections from reviews of silent and sound movies which
I have written for the past few years for a fanzine which I
contribute to the DAPA-EM mailings. They will give you some
idea of how I see films and write about them. They may also
be considered as random notes from an interpretative history
of "reel mysteries" and an implicit statement of my belief
that the present in any art form gains in perspective when it
is viewed within the tradition it either works in or against.

. . . I would rather talk about two great Fritz Lang serial films
linked together as *The Spies* (1919). The director of the Pittsburgh Film-
Makers had described these to me as being the realization of everything
that French serial director Louis Feuillade had tried to do and the prints
as being so immaculately restored that they made most contemporary American films look like sloppily sophomoric exercises in photography. The
two films were shown back to back, which meant that I sat in front of a
fairly small screen in a very uncomfortable seat for almost four hours.
The first of the films deals with a search for a lost Mayan city with a
fabulous treasure and was so successful that Lang, who had been scheduled
to direct *The Cabinet of Dr. Caligari*, was pulled from that film to direct
a sequel detailing the activities of a secret society of master criminals.
The films are incredibly rich in visual detail with an enormous cast of
characters whose faces succeed one another like a display of fine portraits in an art gallery. The total effect of so much detail is tiring at
the time, but shots keep returning so that while the plot disintegrates
into a series of unrelated sequences, the framing of the scenes and the

brilliant editing are unforgettable. One moment in particular impressed itself on me: a shot of the hero clinging to a narrow rope ladder dangling from a stylish plane, a long shot of spidery lines against a neutral sky that reminded me of the quality of certain illustrations in the book edition of H.G. Wells' *When the Sleeper Wakes*.

Where East Is East (Tod Browning, 1929). The great silent film actor Lon Chaney in one of his last silent screen roles. Chaney plays a trapper of wild animals for circuses and zoos whose only joy is the beautiful Eurasian daughter (Lupe Velez) he has raised after her mother abandoned her husband and child. In one of those ironic coincidences so dear to melodrama, the daughter's fiance meets and is seduced by the girl's mother (Estelle Taylor) plying her trade on the riverboat taking him and Chaney to deliver animals to their purchaser. Chaney manages to separate the two but is horrified to find on his return home that the mother has rejoined her unsuspecting daughter. The climax is a bit much, but the stereotyped characters are played with such skill and the film so economically and atmospherically directed by Browning that this silent programmer is uncommonly satisfying. Not one of Chaney's best roles, but he plays it with impressive skill.

The relevation of Cinevent '79 for me was the silent film classic, *Underworld*. George Bancroft plays a self-confident gangster lord with a beautiful mistress (Evelyn Brent) and an educated, alcoholic friend (Clive Brook) who try to smooth his rough edges and find themselves drawn to one another in the process. The action is blunt and swift, but the genius of this film is in the direction of the actors ("My God, but they had faces then!") and the superb playing of this unlikely trio, the kind of ensemble performance that also contributed greatly to the success of *The Glass Key* and all those other melodramas we doted on before television pulped the genre. There's a final shoot-out that makes similar scenes in 1930's gangster films look like well-laundered exercises in *politesse* and the old melodramatic device of the secret passage is revitalized and made a necessary and believable part of the action. The camera work is remarkable (Sternberg was making great films long before he began to exploit Dietrich), with details that come from an older theatrical tradition that makes most recent melodramas look like uneducated exercises in bumbling. The film was meant to be shown with blue and yellow filters (for night and interior scenes), but this obscured the photographic detail to such an extent that the projectionist abandoned the attempt after about twenty minutes. And anyone who thinks that silent films were primitive should be tied to a chair and forced to watch this and any number of other equally accomplished productions until he admits defeat.

At the 1981 Cenevent in Columbus, there were two films of interest to the mystery film buff: James Whale's 1935 feature, *Remember Last Night?*, featuring Robert Young, beautiful Constance Cummings, Edward Arnold as the police detective with Ed Brophy as his assistant, and Arthur Treacher, playing the quintessential English butler; and Frank Tuttle's *Canary Murder Case* (Paramount, 1929), with William Powell as Philo Vance, the unforgettable Louise Brooks as the murderee, Eugene Pallette as the police sergeant, and assorted suspects played by Jean Arthur, Charles Lane, and James Hall.
The Whale film was made during the year he directed his masterpiece, *The Bride of Frankenstein*, and we all applauded vigorously when Cummings walked into a spooky cellar and whispered, "I feel like the Bride of Frankenstein!" Although this film doesn't have the poetic set design of the horror film, the action takes place in a series of art deco fantasies which must have been enormously seductive to an audience wondering where

the next meal was coming from. The characters were as *fantaisiste* as the sets, consisting of a group of rich, witty upper-crusters who make Nick and Nora Charles look like teetotalers and to whom the program notes refer as "a most charming group of alcoholics." The narrative makes absolutely no sense at all on first viewing (and this comes from someone who has never found *The Big Sleep* that confusing) and is mostly an excuse for a group of attractive, talented actors to play outrageously decadent characters in stunning sets and a stoned plot. Arnold and Brophy are an engaging pair, while Young and Cummings play the Powell-Loy roles, with considerably fewer witty lines and no characters to latch onto. Well, they're handsome and talented and there is always Arthur Treacher. I had always enjoyed Treacher for the polish of his performance, but if there is anything distinctly Whalean about this film it must be in the concept of this character, which is almost as eccentric and original as that of Dr. Praetorius in *The Bride*. Treacher is the perfect butler, but he despises his employers and the comments we eavesdrop on are delivered with all the panache of an Olivier or Gielgud in a Restoration romp. I liked this for its look, its eccentricity, and for Treacher. It's crowded, busy, and overly inventive, perhaps, but it may be all the more interesting because of that.

   The Canary Murder Case is the first of the Philo Vance films I have seen. The date is 1929, a wretched year for movies as movie-makers tried to adapt to sound, and it's one of those films that had first been made as a silent and then was redone as it became apparent that sound was really there to stay. Visually, *Canary* is not a very striking film, but it has at least two sizable assets: Powell's polished, intelligent portrayal of VAnce, and the "look" of Louise Brooks, who had a short but notable career and was one of the most beautiful and exciting women in film. Early sound films, or at least the ones I have seen, are very stagy, with every movement calculated and speeches delivered in a slow, "dramatic" fashion. One has the impression that everything is being re-peat-ed for the pub-lic. Powell is unusual in that his style is very restrained and almost casual, so that the camera appears to be eavesdropping on his performance. The detection gimmick that Vance uses is a poker game during which Vance studies all the suspects for clues in their playing style which will reveal to him the one who could have conceived and executed the crime. The problem for me with this gimmick--which I think is an interesting one--is that I don't play poker and couldn't really tell what was going on. Vance's eventual analysis of the players is, I think, sound, but I'm not sure that the film exploited this device as clearly as it might or whether it was just my ignorance of the game. I am tempted to read the novel to see if the fictional character is as attractive as Powell's film persona and also to find out if the murderer's ploy (which I won't reveal) is the same in both mediums. It struck me that the ploy was a kind of metaphor or pun, particularly appropriate for the new medium of sound. That rather excited me, and it works in a way in the sound film that it could not have worked in the silent version.

You Only Live Once (1937). Dir: Fritz Lang. Stars: Henry Fonda, Sylvia Sidney.
This film has been remade twice, most recently and memorably by Robert Altman as *Thieves Like Us*, but the original still impresses as perhaps the most distinctive and powerful of Lang's American films, with a surprising performance by Fonda, who sheds his home-spun, easy-going manner to communicate intensity and even malevolency. Visually, the film has the angular, crepuscular look of German expressionism. One detail in particular lingers in my mind's eye: a shot of two eyes peering from a curtained and partially opened car window, which suggests a masked serial villain of extraordinary intensity threatening the audience with his unblinking

stare. Somehow in this moment is concentrated the idea of an implacable fate tracking the protagonists to their tragic ends.

A film which I think any mystery buff would enjoy is Marcel Carné's 1937 comedy, *Drole de Drame* (released in this country as *Bizarre, Bizarre*). The cast is a superb one, with Louis Jouvet, Michel Simon, Jean-Louis Barrault, Francoise Rosay, and a nice job by a very young Jean-Pierre Aumont. The music is by the ubiquitous Maurice Jaubert (whose music from the 1930's was used most effectively by Francois Truffaut in *The Story of Adele H...*), and the plot turns on a spoof of mystery fiction in which a writer of mystery stories (the great Michel Simon) becomes involved in a "real life" mystery fiction. It's farcical and, at times, too frantic but most entertaining. One word of warning: the titles are sometimes white against white, and the print I saw was not the cleanest.

The Glass Key (Dir.: Stewart Heisler, 1942) is one of those tight, brilliantly photographed and acted genre films that Hollywood used to turn out before it got a severe case of the bloats in the early fifties, an affliction from which it has yet to recover. Veronica Lake and Alan Ladd were a playful pair of wary lovers, but the best acting was by the secondary players, with *Life of Riley* bumblebrain William Bendix very impressive as a dullwitted hooligan with a pair of brutal fists spoiling for a bit of sadistic fun. In the most extended sequence, Ladd is thoroughly worked over by Bendix and a sidekick in a sleazy backroom that climaxes in a spectacular escape that is as well-edited as anything you are ever likely to see in a film. Good acting also by Brian Donlevy, Joseph Calleia, Minor Watson, and others, and one of those petulant, imature bad-girl roles that Bonita Granville specialized in before she went to the dogs with the Lassie series. I revelled in the crisp photography, the economical dialogue, the tight pacing and editing, and the sexual teasing that went on between Ladd and Lake. Meryl Streep has some of the look of Lake and, while Lake may not be as subtle an actress, she has real class and, legend to the contrary, she does have a right profile which she shows to great advantage in this classic private-eye *film-noir*.

And, lest it be thought that I am hopelessly committed to living in the past, I will recommend *Sharky's Machine*, in which a narcotics detective (Burt Reynolds) is shipped down to the seamy confines of the vice squad after a bungled set-up in which a civilian is killed. Nobody knew how to get out of the plot improbabilities, but until that botched ending you may appreciate the sensational screen debut of husky-voiced Rachel Ward and the good acting of a team of supporting players, marred only by one of those caricatural, hysterical performances that Charles Durning has been giving us of late. There is one stunning pan up the side of a modernistic tower glittering like an Arabian Nights palace. That is the kind of entertaining film that I would never pay $4 for but which pleases me at the $1.50 matinees I attend.

(Continued from page 20) titling," which was immediately followed, at the top of page 123, by another table on "Approximate word count in THE SHADOW novels." Finally, half way down page 123, we get to the examples the "Thus:" at the top of the preceeding page refers to.

In another place someone mis-keyed the typesetter and an entire paragraph was printed in italics. In another, footnotes appear not at the foot of the page where they belong, but in-
(Continued on page 31)

Judgments

More Movie Reviews
By Jim Traylor

The Glass Key (1942).   Director: Stuart Heisler.   Screenplay:
Jonathan Latimer.   From the novel by Dashiell Hammett.

This Veronica Lake—Alan Ladd vehicle was the second film
version of Hammett's novel. (The first was done in 1935.)
The plot involves the corruption of the reform candidate for
governor in an unnamed state.
Alan Ladd portrays Ed Beaumont, the assistant to the head
of the Voters' League, Paul Madvig (played by Brian Donlevy).
The story opens with Madvig deciding to back the Reform Party's
candidate, Ralph Henry, hinting that even a reform candidate
can be corrupted. Henry's daughter, Janet (Veronica Lake),
overhears Madvig's slur, slaps him quite hard, and gives him a
verbal dressing down. Madvig's reaction is to say "What a
slugger!" and immediately fall in love with her.
Madvig tells Ed Beaumont that Henry is just as good as in
his pocket and has practically given him the key to the Henry
house. Ed responds soberly: "A glass key. . . . Careful it
doesn't break off in your hands." But good advice is seldom
followed in mystery/suspense films. Madvig's aim is to get
the same power on the state level that he already enjoys
locally. The D.A. is already on his payroll, and Madvig
figures that the governor would make a nice "friend." In an
effort to appear honest and at the same time show his support
for Henry, Madvig decides to close down a local gambling club
belonging to Nick Varna. Varna has been paying protection
money to Madvig, and he is understandably upset by the closing.
Matters are complicated by the fact that Henry's gambling
and spendthrift son, Taylor, is in debt to Varna and is the
lover of Madvig's eighteen-year-old sister, Opal. Taylor
Henry is played by Richard Denning--later famous as the Mister
of *Mr. and Mrs. North*--and Opal is played by Bonita Granville;
both are superficial characters. Trying to help Taylor out of
one of his never-ending jams over gambling debts, Opal borrows
$500 from Ed Beaumont and promptly turns it over to her lover.
Beaumont follows her to Taylor's apartment and practically
drags her away to Madvig's place. Once Madvig learns that
she's seeing Taylor, he rushes out making threatening remarks
about him. Opal gets Ed to follow Madvig, and Ed finds Taylor's dead body lying in the street in front of Henry's man-
sion.
Nick Varna, now Madvig's enemy, has his hooks into Clyde

Mathews, the owner of the local paper, and he forces the *Observer* to begin printing accusations that Madvig killed Taylor Henry. A further complication involves an anonymous letter received by District Attorney Farr (Donald MacBride) which asks the question, "If Paul Madvig didn't kill Taylor Henry, how did his best friend happen to find the body?"

Beaumont and Janet Henry are attracted to each other, but Beaumont remains loyal to his friend, calling him "a straight-up guy." He eventually decided that the only way to "save" Madvig is to pick a fight with him and then infiltrate Varna's gang as Madvig's ex-friend. Once there, he destroys an affidavit signed by Sloss (Dane Clark), a disgruntled ex-employee who actually saw Taylor Henry and Paul Madvig that night on the street where the body was found. An enraged Varna delegates two hoods to work Ed over. One, named Jeff (William Bendix), is extremely sadistic. Each time he sees Ed he taunts him: "Buddy, you sure are one for getting beat up."

After Ed escapes from this beating, Sloss is shot down in the street and Opal goes away for the weekend to Clyde Mathews' place to give an exclusive interview to the *Observer* declaring that she believes her brother killed Taylor Henry. Ed again goes to rescue her. There he reveals to Mathews' wife Eloise that the paper is going broke and that her husband is in Varna's pocket. Eloise immediately begins to make a play for Ed. The resulting trauma is too much for Mathews. He becomes depressed and commits suicide.

The success of the film depends on how much the viewer believes in the credibility of Ed Beaumont as a character. He behaves as would any ordinary citizen whose best friend is accused of murder. Madvig confounds things by not telling the truth about the situation, and Ed is left to his own devices to clear Madvig. He figures out the significance of the anonymous notes and uses that knowledge to identify the real murderer.

Among the prime suspects is Janet Henry. Ed has tried to keep his feelings for her to himself because he knows that Madvig loves her (in his way). Ladd and Lake share a number of sultry scenes. In one, Janet Henry is trying to discover if Madvig killed her brother. She goes alone to Ed's apartment, and, with the camera showing off that lovely profile and long silver hair, asks Ed:

--"You don't like me, do you, Mr. Beaumont?"

--"I think I do."

In another scene, Janet has decided that she should make a play for Ed, but he again rebuffs her. His loyalty to Madvig is quite strong. He would stand by him even if he'd killed Taylor.

Once Ed has cleared Madvig, there's a good scene in which Ed and Janet finally decide that they love each other. Madvig enters Ed's apartment as they are kissing and soon gives them his blessing, all the while taking back the engagement ring which he gave Janet. He leaves whistling. Madvig, of course, never loved Janet as much as he loved the power which her father could give him.

There's one scene which, although it doesn't add much to the flow of the film, certainly stands out in the dimension of *film noir*. In it, Ed is trying to trick information from the hood Jeff. Varna has told Jeff to stay out of sight, but Ed has traced him to the seediest of seedy bars. Jeff is thrilled;

29

he sees another opportunity to beat up on Ed. Varna surprises
Jeff and knows that Ed was just trying to get information.
Varna and Ed talk as if Jeff were not in the room. Jeff gets
mad and makes a run at Varna. In the fight, Ed comes up with
the gun. As soon as he sees this, Jeff says:
  --"Got the roscoe?"
  --"Yes."
  --"You see what we got to do! We got to give him the
  works!"
Everyone, including Jeff, thinks that the only solution is
murder, but Ed is not that sort. At the end of the film he's
leaving for better things; he's through with crooked politics
and all that it entails.
    The amusing aspect of the fight between Varna and Jeff is
the use of the word roscoe. Calling a gun a roscoe reminds
the viewer of Dan Turner, Hollywood Detective, Robert L. Bel-
lem's fast-punning P.I. of the West Coast. In a movie which
is consistently somber, it's a welcome comic touch.
    The movie delivers good entertainment. My only qualm is
that it leaves unstated its position toward the corruption of
Paul Madvig. But perhaps it's just a realistic presentation
of the absolute power of politics.

Sharky's Machine (1981). Director: Burt Reynolds. Screenplay:
    Geraldo Di Pego. From the novel by William Diehl.

    Sharky's Machine illustrates the difficulty of adapting a
long adventure/suspense novel to the screen. Diehl's novel
spans two-and-a-half decades and three continents; Reynolds'
movie covers about two weeks and involves only the local re-
gion around Atlanta, Georgia.
    Still, *Sharky's Machine* is a powerful action picture.
Reynolds tries to solve the problem of the varied plot devices
by presenting a few short scenes involving each of the nefar-
ious characters. The audience, for example, perceives that
gubernatorial candidate Hotchkins (Earl Holliman) is a corrupt
politician funded by international crime boss Victor (Vittorio
Gassman). But this knowledge comes fairly late in the picture,
only after the rapid movement of the early part of the film
has slowed with a tedious stakeout of a $1000-a-night call
girl, Dominoe (Rachel Ward). Along the way, the audience is
treated to several bloody killings by a drug-crazed psychopath
who is rather confusingly revealed as Victor's brother.
    The good scenes involve Sharky (Burt Reynolds) in action
sequences or in character interaction with the members of the
vice squad, his "machine" (Brian Keith, Charles Durning, Bernie
Casey, and Richard Libertini), to which he is demoted after a
drug bust goes bad and an innocent bystander is murdered. Up
until the time the vice squad discovers a list of coded phone
numbers (Dominoe's is just one of seven), the film is fast-
paced and quite entertaining. The violence is not quite so
evident in the first half of the picture, and character development is adequate for the audience to really care about
the machine.
    Then, director Reynolds allows the picture to slow as he
concentrates on Sharky's attachment to Dominoe. For fifteen
tedious minutes the camera follows Dominoe. Unfortunately,
the ravishingly beautiful Rachel Ward (looking remarkably

similar to a young Jacqueline Bisset) is not presented during
these scenes to her best advantage. As for plot development,
surely one or two scenes in which the machine is shown staking
out her apartment would be sufficient to establish that Dominoe
is a call girl. It is only after Victor discovers that Dominoe
wants to leave him and become Hotchkins' mistress that the
picture begins to move again. His decision to have her killed
instills new movement. However, the psycho killer is shown,
quite unbelievably, staking out Dominoe's apartment from the
same floor of the building in which Sharky's machine is operating.
    The action fairly reeks of being shot for TV. The scenes
could be used almost completely with blips of some objection-
able dialogue and blood. There are basically no sex scenes
between Sharky and Dominoe. Instead, director Reynolds concentrates on embarrassingly hokey dialogue and long, lingering
looks. His emphasis on violence is not really excessive, but
it is not balanced with equally sharp non-violent scenes. The
final minutes of the movie, in which Sharky's machine tracks
down the psycho killer, are exciting, but they are extremely
bloody and, for a police movie, unrealistic in the sense that
there is no logical reason for so many people to be shot chasing down one hop-head.
    The film is enjoyable but is by no means a classic. It
has the great good fortune of being released in a year in
which there are few good movies. It is among the best of the
current films, but it is flawed and positively screams for re-
editing.

Rollover (1981). Director: Alan J. Pakula.

    Compared to this movie, *Sharky's Machine* is a veritable
work of art. Jane Fonda and Kris Kristofferson star in this
combination mystery/financial-doomsday thriller. The film begins effectively with the murder of Jane's financier husband
in his posh office in New York's World Trade Center. Unfortunately, the action soon shifts from this mystery story--who
killed the husband? why is the Casper Milquetoast bank examin-
er behaving mysteriously? and how was he able to buy that
fancy new house?--to the equally mysterious (and just as un-
fathomable) world of an Arab plot to corner the entire world's
gold supply.
    Hume Cronyn has sent Kristofferson into a small brokerage
house, ostensibly to save it from financial ruin. It becomes
apparent that Cronyn merely wants the company to stay alive
long enough for its Arab assets to be slowly converted to gold
and transferred to his much larger banking firm. The "rollover" of the title refers to the financial arrangement by
which huge sums of money in American banks are reinvested
(rolled over) at their maturity dates instead of being with-
drawn. The term also has a sexual connotation, for Fonda and
Kristofferson quickly become an item. One of the few funny
lines in the movie occurs when Jane and Kris arrive late at a
dinner party. Says Kris: "Sorry, we just made it."
    They might have, but the film doesn't. From this point,
the action either is not followed through or becomes direction-
less. The murder of Jane's husband is allowed to go unsolved
while the major emphasis of the movie shifts to the possibility

of world economic collapse when the Arabs refuse to rollover
their assets and demand immediate withdrawal of their funds.
The ensuing banking collapse is made to resemble the stock
market crash of 1929, complete with bankers blowing their
brains out in high-rise offices.

Rollover is a smooth, slick movie with a few good scenes
and some credible acting, but in the final view the action
takes too many unbelievable turns. Pakula, usually a quite
reliable director, does not give the film the firm control it
needs. He never seems to make up his mind what he wants to
do with his several plots. All the players are good; the plot
devices just cheat them.

Murder Is Easy (1982). Director: Claude Whatham. Teleplay:
    Carmen Culver. From the story by Agatha Christie. Broad-
    cast 2 January 1982 on CBS-TV.

Fans of Lesley-Anne Down (Georgina in PBS's biggest hit,
Upstairs, Downstairs) finally got to see her in a decent vehicle. Those of us who suffered through that awful car picture and then *Sphinx* were at last treated to Miss Down in her
element. In this Agatha Christie story she plays Bridget Con-
way, secretary and fiancee to Lord Gordon Easterfield (Timothy
West). She subsequently falls in love with a vacationing
American, Luke Williams (Bill Bixby), who comes to the small
town of Wychwood-under-Ashe. Luke had met Miss Lavinia Fullerton (a nice cameo by Helen Hayes) on a train ride on Derby
Day. Miss Fullerton is traveling to London to notify Scotland
Yard of a series of accidents which she considers to be murder.
Luke, a professor and author (of *Probability and Chance*), becomes interested in her wildly improbable tale only after she
is killed in a car accident only minutes after the train's
arrival in London.

Miss Fullerton's one great line keeps ringing in Luke's
head: "So long as no one suspects you, murder is easy." Luke
feels compelled to go to Miss Fullerton's home town and try to
make an investigation. It's a nice touch for Christie fans
that Luke is not a people-person. He's just broken off a
relationship with his girlfriend because she cannot live with
his impersonal nature. It's a form of therapy for Luke to
investigate the murder. It involves him for the first time
with people as individuals and not as mere numbers. This
commitment to the memory of Miss Fullerton even leads to his
falling in love with Bridget.

As usual in films based on Christie stories, a number of
red herrings and false leads abound. There's no real danger
here; just enjoyment. For this viewer--who much prefers the
film adaptations of Miss Christie's stories to the prose versions (except, perhaps, for the masterpiece *And Then There
Were None*)--the film is quite enjoyable, well played by attractive players. *Murder Is Easy* is good, clean fun. Catch
the rerun.

(Continued from page 26) terspersed randomly throughout the
text. Then there's the problem of arbitrary margins and ir-
ratic indentations, and indented quotations being printed in
the same size and type as the body of the text, and .... It
(Continued on page 37)

Mystery*File

Short Reviews by Steve Lewis

Jonathan Valin. *Final Notice*. Dodd, Mead, 1980, 246 pp.

I'm a little behind. This is the second adventure of private eye Harry Stoner--it's just now in paperback--and the third is already out, begging to be read.
The metaphor is apt. If anything, I found this one even more readable than *The Lime Pit*, which started to get more and more funny-tasting the deeper Stoner began to dig into the corruption surrounding the city of Cincinnati.
There is some of the same in this one, plus lots of gore. Stoner is called in when a psychopath starts slashing up nudes in a library's collection of art books. He thinks it's only a prelude to a real killing. At his side on this case is a library security guard named Kate Davis, who is both female and liberated.
Stoner feels old and tired at thirty-seven, old-fashioned and chauvinistic. Kate is of a younger generation, and falling in love with her leaves Stoner feeling slightly bewildered. He is also pleased.
Valin has a fine feeling for what makes people what they are--not just the killer, but everyone. The constant attempts to psychoanalyze the killer could have been downplayed a little, and Valin doesn't quite catch the same edge that exists between human relationships that Robert B. Parker usually does, but as a mixture of character study and action adventure, it is seldom done any better than this.
The fast and furious climax works out almost the way you'd expect it to, but the twist that comes with it just might catch you leaning the wrong way. (A minus)

James Anderson. *Assault and Matrimony*. Doubleday/Crime Club, 1981 (first published in 1980), 185 pp., $10.95.

On the surface, Sylvia and Edgar Chambers have a marriage that is too good to be true. In fact, it isn't. Unknown to either, each hates the other with a passion, and it takes only a nudge to send them both completely over the edge.
The comedy of errors that quickly follows is deeply tinged in black. Each of these two basically unlikeable people tries in fierce desperation to kill the other--and any innocent bystanders who happen to be wandering by--and yet neither of

32

them quite manages to succeed. There is not an ounce of con-
science between them.
    It would not be at all difficult for the easily disillu-
sioned reader to become completely exasperated with both of
them, giving up with disgust at the seemingly endless variety
of their elaborately structured plots. Fortunately, the ending is even more clever and complex, surpassing anything
either of them has come up with before then.
    It's a challenge, but it's also well worth the wait. (B
plus)* (*Reviews so marked have appeared earlier in the Hart-
ford *Courant*.)

[Agatha Christie]. *Agatha Christie: The Art of Her Crimes*.
    The Paintings of Tom Adams, with a Commentary by Julian
    Symons. Everest House, 1981, 144 pp., $24.95.

    Paperback cover art reaches a new high with this deluxe
hardcover edition of over ninety Tom Adams paintings, all done
for various editions of Agatha Christie's mysteries, both in
this country and in Britain.
    Those expecting numerous repeated portrayals of Miss Marple
and Hercule Poirot, two of Christie's most well-known detective
characters, will come away disappointed, however. Adams leans
more to the symbolic and to surrealism in his work, and the
commentary provided by both himself and by noted mystery critic
Julian Symons reveals just how many clues he managed to work
into the overall design of each of the covers here.
    Tastes in art being what they are, it is amusing to note
that one of the paintings Adams considers one of his best,
Symons slides over as nothing out of the ordinary.
    The subject matter of Christie's works being what it is,
it is not surprising that the overall effect is rather a dour
one--lots of skulls, bloody instruments, and other paraleph-
nalia of murder. Nevertheless, given the double-barrelled
insights into the works of perhaps the most famous mystery
writer of all time, Agatha Christie's many fans will find this
more than a must for browsing through.

Thomas Mahon. *The Fandango Involvement*. Fawcett Gold Medal,
    1981, 221 pp., $2.25.

    Here's a curious little book, one so far off the beaten
path--especially as a mystery, although the evidence indicates
that the author may have intended it to be something more than
that--that without actually having it in hand it's hard to
consider its ever being thought publishable.
    Billy Fandango is a dwarf with a lot of curiosity. A fel-
low employee at the company for which he's a computer expert
seems to live in agonized total isolation and to have aged
years beyond his time. Why?
    Just as this man seems to be coming out of his shell, he
commits suicide. Or is it? Naturally, Billy and his six-foot
girlfriend decide that further investigation is in order.
    As I say, this is an unusual book, and so's the ending,
involving both Vietnam and the arms industry--and isn't it
strange to realize that Vietnam is now very nearly ancient
history? But the whole affair is still strangely out of kil-

ter. The story line reels and staggers like the proverbial
drunken sailor, this way and that, and back again.
It's also overwritten by at least half a notch, with some
of the worst of the flowery dialogue sounding as if it came
straight from the pages of the latest Marvel comic book. It's
the best of its field, I grant you, but by no stretch of the
imagination could anyone ever be considered as actually talk-
ing that way.) (C)

Loren D. Estleman. *Angel Eyes*. Houghton Mifflin, 1981,
203 pp., #11.95.

Like all good private eyes, Amos Walker is a man with an
unswervable code of honor. When his client, a girl singer
with unforgettable eyes, disappears, as she had predicted she
would, shaking him from the case is as easy as sneaking a
steak from a hungry dog.
The scene is Detroit, and union politics combine with and
merge into the inevitable background of a city in slow decay.
To perk things up and to keep the case moving, Estleman is a
present master of the well-tuned metaphor.
He is also better at mood than he is at plot, and there is
enough plot in the second half of the story to choke a full-
grown horse. The longer the trail becomes, the more it in-
sists on turning incestuously back upon itself.
Not surprisingly, there are also plenty of guns to go
around. (B minus)*

Laird Koenig. *Rockabye*. St. Martin's, 1981, 246 pp., $11.95.

Novels of the occult and the supernatural are tremendously
popular today, and part of the reason has to be the excuses
they give people for avoiding the real world, the one they
have to live in.
Considering the unspeakable things that can happen to a kidnapped two-year-old boy in New York City at Christmas time,
here's a book that will scare the heck out of just about
everyone, and get them back to reading about witches and demons
and the like.
In part, the police are also the villains in this one,
giving up too easily on what they think is just another un-
solvable crime. The boy's mother, a traveler alone in the
city, nevertheless refuses to concede defeat. Her only assist-
ance comes from a sympathetic female newspaper reporter and an
aging psychic-for-hire whom she really believes to be a fraud.
Screenwriter Laird Koenig has an unerring eye for situations easily translatable into cinematic magic. You can expect to see it on a screen near you very soon.
The mayor of New York City won't like it, nor will police
departments anywhere in the country. I can't say that I'd
blame them in the slightest. (C plus)*

Henry Wade. *The Hanging Captain*. Perennial Library, 1981
(first published in 1933), 301 pp., $2.50.

Henry Wade is as unlikely an author as you could expect to
find in your local paperback bookstore, and thanks should go

to whoever at Perennial is responsible for seeing to it that
he is. Who knows, maybe even John Rhode will be next!
What Wade does best, at least in this particular example
of his work, is to demonstrate that there is no reason why a
good, solid detective story must also be dull. There is a lot
of importance placed upon alibis and time-tables in this case,
and with some splendid cooperation between Scotland Yard and
the local police the murderer of Sir Herbert Sterron is inevitably brought to justice.
*WARNING: While I trust that I can safely keep the identity
of the killer a secret in the discussion that follows, exper-
ienced mystery readers may discern important aspects of the
solution of the crime that they'd really rather not know.*
I am curious that the dead man's mysterious affliction was
never mentioned. In *A Catalogue of Crime*, Barzun and Taylor
tell us it was syphilis, but it might be noted that it was the
English edition that they read.
This one fact explains a good deal. For example, it gives
us the reason for Captain Sterron's mysterious withdrawal from
society some years before. And, what is more, it also adds a
strong tinge of irony to the killer's motive--the overriding
reason he did what he did.
I have to wonder how much alteration was done to the American version, which I assume this edition follows. From all
accounts, Wade was an intelligent writer, and, although I know
little about him otherwise, I am surprised that he passed up a
fine opportunity to make the final crushing blow that this one
would have been. (B plus)

Brad Latham. *The Hook #1: The Gilded Canary*. Warner, 1981,
174 pp., $1.95.

Warner has been publishing books in several of its various
new "Men of Action" series for some time now, and for mystery
fans here is the first appearance of the one that might seem
the most promising. "The Hook" is Bill Lockwood, a 1930's
private eye who is as tough with his fists as he is energetic
in bed.
There seems to be little else to say. Lockwood's case, as
he investigates the theft of some jewelry from a rich girl
singer named Muffy Dearborn, is nothing less than a flimsy
excuse for him to jump in and out of a bed or two and beat up
a few hoodlums with his patented left hook.
There are a few good moments--once in a while I did get a
fleeting impression that there was some intelligent thought
put into the writing of this mediocre excuse for a book--but
they quickly pass.
It's probably exactly what Warner had in mind. (D)

Garrity [David James Gerrity]. *Kiss off the Dead*. Gold Medal,
1960, 140pp.

To get the sour taste of the Hook book out of my head, I
immediately went to my collection of prime Gold Medal stock
and more or less picked this one out at random. I've read
enough of these early paperback gems to be convinced that the
booze-babes-and-bullets approach to detective/mystery fiction

does not automatically have to mean that it's a lousy book.

To tell you the truth, I was still a little worried for a while. Could it be that I was wrong, that my memory had gone bad? After reading this, though, my doubts were gone. I was completely reassured. They just don't write 'em the way they used to, that's all there is to it.

This is the story of Max Carey, an ex-cop who's gone bad, on the trail of a woman, his wife, who is to blame--a tramp, although he refuses to admit it, even to himself. Just as he finds her--in a smoke-filled bar on the way to Florida--she disappears again, and her body turns up in the ocean the next day.

Small-town cops being what they are, Carey is blamed, and he spends the rest of the book one step ahead of the law--and the mob--desperately trying to find the killer before either one of them finds him. A hat-check girl named Sherry is the only person who is on his side.

Not a terrifically original plot, I have to admit, but Garrity's roughly-hewed writing style is still alive, even to the point of being almost poetically effective in papering over the clichés. The non-stop action includes the pre-requisite bedroom scene, but here at least the camera pulls away before the flickering X-rating light goes flashing on.

The book is filled with as much lust for blood as the Warner book, if not more, but what Garrity does that Latham doesn't is to make you feel it--as a participant, if you will, not a voyeur. (B)

Margaret Millar. *Mermaid*. Morrow, 1982, 215 pp., $11.50.

Tom Aragon, whose position as a junior member of a pres-tigious Southern California law firm has him largely doing legwork for the senior members, occasionally has the oppor-tunity of adding detective duties to his list of chores. He's no expert at it, by any means, but for an amateur he does pretty well.

This case has to do with a runaway girl--which comes as no surprise, since the west coast must be full of them--but with a difference. Cleo Jasper is a member of a very wealthy fam-ily, she is pretty, if not beautiful, and she is exceptional. Mildly retraded, that is, and just beginning to become aware of her "rights."

As in all good drama, the characters in Millar's panoramic novels are often a mysterious mixture of the comic with the tragic. While she does not realize it, unfortunately, Cleo Jasper is the supreme archetype of each. (A)*

Joyce Harrington. *No One Knows My Name*. Avon, 1980, 239 pp., $2.25.

An alternative title might have been *Death Comes to Duck Lake*, a small former fishing community up near Traverse City, Michigan--my kind of country. I know it well.

On the other hand, I can see where actor- and actressy-types from Hollywood and New York City--in this case, budding ones or those over the hill--might think of Duck Lake as the ultimate of boondocks. Still, when the repertory company for

the hamlet's summer playhouse makes them the only job offer
they can get, somehow it has to start looking not quite so
bad, after all.

But one of this year's company is a compulsive murderer,
willing to kill to keep anyone else from the inevitable disappointments due them from choosing one of the most fickle
careers of them all--show business.

Except for the fact that there is no one here to fill the
role of the eccentric detective character, this is truly a
classic harkening back to the Golden Age of Mysteries. If
there isn't an overabundance of physical clues, there are lots
of hidden secrets and ominous hints and lots of suspects busily
mucking up the evidence.

The end, as an aging actor makes a tragically wrong decision, is a deeply chilling one. Indeed, in its way, it's a
completely perfect one. (A)

(Continued from page 31) is, taken all together, a book-lover's
nightmare, and I am sure the greatest sufferer of all is Bob
Sampson himself. He didn't get to see the page proofs before
the book went to press, so these faults are not attributable
to him. Yet it's Bob's name, not that of the anonymous per-
petrator of these misdeeds, that's on the book, and Bob is the
one that will get the blame. And that just isn't fair; it's
tough enough having to live with one's own mistakes, without
being saddled with those of others.

But--miraculously--as bad and distracting as these flaws
are, they do not succeed in sinking Bob's work, which is
strong enough to carry the load. For all the sins committed
against it, *The Night Master* is still a first-rate history of
one of the most interesting characters to come out of the
pulps, and Bob's work is well worth the teeth-grinding and
fist-clinching a reader has to go through to read it. Do not
let these criticisms keep you from buying this book.

BILL PRONZINI'S SCATTERSHOT

Bill Pronzini's latest novel, *Scattershot* (St. Martin's,
$10.95), arrived yesterday, and I'm going to make these al-
ready over-long editorial remarks even longer in order to comment on it in this issue, since it has a release date of 26
April. Like at least one of Bill's previous novels, this is
really just three short stories linked together by an overlaid
connective narrative. Each of the separate stories involves
an "impossible" crime, and the unnamed detective solves all
three with precise logic which, unfortunately, can only have
been derived from divine inspiration. To put it another way,
the solutions which the P.I. posits fit all the facts, but any
number of other solutions could do the same. (Of course,
Bill's protagonist has the advantage of taking on only criminals who can't restrain themselves from confessing and con-
firming all his conclusions as soon as he reveals them.) Now
this is fine in short stories, where limitations of time and
space prevent more detailed and convincing proofs, but in what
purports to be a novel such failings are quite jarring.

Having said all that, it is my pleasure to be able to add
that I enjoyed the book very much. Given a choice between a

(Continued on page 47)

Verdicts

More Reviews

Anna Clarke. *Letter from the Dead*. Doubleday, 1981.

Anna Clarke's view of human nature is grim. The characters in her novels are flawed human beings whose personal
limitations are exacerbated by the intrusion of murder, often
of their own doing. Her most recent novel, *Letter from the
Dead,* doesn't vary that pattern by an inch; what it does do,
however, is vary the high degree of skill and inventiveness
its author has displayed heretofore; *Letter* is less ably done,
less demanding of its readers than Clarke's earlier novels.
Clarke fans will certainly want to read it, but it is not the
best introduction to her work for newcomers.
    The chief problem here is that the characters are not so
clearly depicted as usual. The plot revolves around young
Clive Bradley's determination to prove that his hateful step-
father murdered his mother. Complications include a missing
deathbed letter, a deathbed confession, the personal and pro-
fessional problems of the local vicar, Nevil Gray, and his
tart-tongued daughter, Angela, and the not-very-hard-to-solve
mystery of the illegitimate Clive's true parentage. None of
these elements is very new or different, but they do have
tried and proved potential. Usually, in the hands of Anna
Clarke they would realize that potential, but this time they
miss. Generally, readers come to know Clarke's characters
very well, come to identify with them, and enjoy the books
because the stories cast a clear, steady light on traits in
the human personality which we regret but recognize all too
well. Here, identification is missing because no character
comes fully alive; Clarke's characteristic shifts in point of
view (she tells her tales in third person, but takes readers
into the minds of various characters) simply are not revealing
enough. Clive, Nevil, and Angela, as well as several minor
characters, especially Ronnie Fenwick, Nevil's curate, are
rich lodes left unmined.
    One chapter begins with a sardonic description of one of
Nevil's regular services:

> Evensong at St. Mark's, Southdene, was usually well attended.
> ... Nevil never preached for long and often said things that
> made you want to laugh and he didn't seem to mind if you did
> laugh. It ... left people feeling a little less gloomy about
> the state of the world and a little more willing to tolerate

people they were annoyed with--for a few hours at any rate.

Letter from the Dead may well have much the same effect. It won't make you laugh, but it will take your mind off the economy for a few hours and it might make you temporarily a bit more tolerant, for this novel resolves itself into a tight, tidy, happy ending--a very sharp departure from the open-ended, thoughtful, even disquiting but *realistic* resolution of most of Clarke's efforts. Most of her novels are memorable, offering ideas and insights for long-term, thoughtful contemplation; *Letter* offers a few hours of distraction. For an author who has the potential to give genuine sustenance, this snack isn't quite good enough. (Jane S. Bakerman)

Lillian O'Donnell. *The Children's Zoo*. Putnam's, 1981.

In *The Children's Zoo*, Lillian O'Donnell's intriguing continuing characters, Norah Mulcahaney and her husband, Joe Capretto, are going through a strained period; their marriage remains stable, but differences in opinion about Norah's next career step and about her intense desire to be a mother--even a surrogate mother--generate considerable tension. O'Donnell would be a far lesser craftsperson than she is were she to ignore the potential difficulty arising from two officers of the law trying to accommodate their marriage to their careers, and here she confronts those difficulties with considerable honesty and success.
Norah is growing with her job, a feature of the novels which brings satisfaction to O'Donnell fans. Earlier in her service as a New York City cop, Norah ran afoul of corruption, reported it, and has been carrying a burden of some isolation and--oddly but very humanly--some guilt ever since. In *The Children's Zoo*, she once again uncovers a colleague's illegal practices; this time, she confronts the situation personally, attempting to serve her sense of justice and honor without besmirching the force or invoking the cumbersome internal affairs system. This subplot demonstrates, as do several other incidents in *Zoo*, that Norah is gaining confidence, learning to play the game and to compromise with the letter of the law. The pattern recalls dozens of other police procedurals but remains, nevertheless, fresh and viable.
The main plot of *The Children's Zoo* revolves around Norah's difficult and partially unauthorized investigation of a series of dreadful crimes perpetrated by teenagers. The irony of an officer so intent upon becoming a parent having to face the genuine evil the youngsters involved represent is never lost upon the reader, though it is never exploited by O'Donnell. Nor, of course, is the rather heavy and ominous irony of the title. O'Donnell's vision of the future of our culture--or at least of our major cities, which can be taken as a powerful symbol of American society--seems to be darkening with every book.
The Children's Zoo is a partially flawed effort--one wishes O'Donnell had done her research a bit more carefully. She speaks of some mysterious eye fluid at one point (surely the proper name or names would have been easily established), and her brief, bitter comparison of young criminals of this century to youth gangs which terrorized medieval cities is too super-

ficial. If it's important enough to include, it's important enough to treat carefully, and that fact is not excused by the ruse used here--the historical information is supposedly the result of a few hurried hours of reading Norah does in the public library. That kind of skimming over the surface doesn't belong in a major novel by a good crime writer.

Nevertheless, O'Donnell is polishing her craft; Norah is developing nicely, and the portraits of various youngsters are stunning. These factors outweigh the flaws. Lillian O'Donnell's *Children's Zoo* is well worth reading. (Jane S. Bakerman)

Mark Derby. *Afraid in the Dark*. Viking, 1952 (first published in Britain as *Malayan Rose*, Collins, 1951), 280pp.

During the 1950's and 1960's, several British writers devoted a number of their books to the subject of intrigue in Southeast Asia. Some, such as Mark Derby, Simon Harvester, and Gavin Black, have become specialists in this small subgenre. The source of the intrigue is usually the threat of communism spreading throughout that area. The tone or theme of many of the books is a post—World War II pessimism and a sense of loss of Empire. *Afraid in the Dark* is perhaps the first, and certainly one of the best, of these.

Patrick Derrex, 29, had volunteered for military service in the East after WWII; he was sent to Java and was tortured by Indonesian nationalists. After four years' recuperation in a British military hospital, he emerges disoriented and lonely. He takes a bus to his childhood home and renews his acquaintance with Rose, who had worked as a maid for his parents when Derrex was living at home. Later, casting about for something to do with his life, Derrex sees a mysterious notice in the paper. Answering it takes him to the house of Captain H.J.H. Irvingham. Irvingham wants someone to go to Malaya to locate and execute an ex-Kempetai official named Makota. Makota had been in charge of the disposal of a number of POWs for the Japanese and had hideously tortured many people, including Irvingham's wife. She is now maimed and crippled for life.

Although Derrex does not want to kill anyone, he takes the commission, and he takes Rose along with him (without telling her exactly why they are going). Once in Singapore, Derrex locates Makota right away, but he must wait for the right circumstances to kill him. Makota, a Scots-Javanese half-caste, is a powerful study in resentment, viciousness, and violence. It does not take Makota long to learn that Derrex is after him, and the resulting battle of wits is suspense at its best.

Derby has a gift for close-focusing on interpersonal situations and psychological suspense. He handles something as trite as the awkward dinner table conversation in a way to make the reader cringe with embarrassment. In another scene there is such a horrifying portrayal of claustrophobia that it was mone of the most gruelling (but suspenseful) reading experiences I have ever had. Derby is even able to merge Derrex's character growth organically with the plot. Finally, the setting is refreshing--there is a smooth transition from the dry English countryside to the steamy jungle overlooking Singapore Harbor. Recommended. (Greg Goode)

[Philip Wylie and Bernard Bergman.] *The Smiling Corpse.* Illustrated by Georg Hartmann. Farrar & Rinehart, 1935,
202 pp.

By 1935 there had already been many book-length studies of
the detective genre in English, French, and German. Dorothy
Sayers' introductions and commentary in her *Great Short Stories
of Detection, Mystery, and Horror*, although not themselves
book length, were valuable and ground-breaking. They appeared
in different volumes and editions five or six times before
1935. Carolyn Wells' *Technique of the Mystery Story* was re-
vised in 1929. Thomson's *Masters of Mystery* appeared in 1931.
There were many others. The time seemed ripe for a tongue-in-
cheek fictional treatment of the genre and its practitioners
and critics.

The subtitle of *The Smiling Corpse* is, "Wherein G.K. Chesterton, S.S. Van Dine, Sax Rohmer, and Dashiell Hammett are
surprised to find themselves at a murder." The victim is one
Wendel Hyat, mystery critic, celebrity, and reputed author of
From Poe to Plethora. At a literary tea given in his honor by
his publishers, the Dunhams, at their posh Park Avenue pent-
house, Hyat is found shot to death in the bathtub. Since Hyat
was a womanizer, an acerbic critic, and an irritating and selfish man, there are many at the tea with motive to kill him.
As the subtitle suggests, among those present are Chesterton,
Van Dine, Rohmer, and Hammett, each of whom wants to solve the
murder and thinks he can do so better than the policial official who happens to be present, Sergeant Michael O'Casey. The
narrator is a sophisticated, slick, likable "cinemactor," John
Graham Ballantine, who talks like a Hammett character.

As Ballantine follows each writer in turn through the
steps of his investigation, the idiosyncracies of style and
character of each writer are caricatured. Hammett skulks
around with a drink in his hand, looking for the murder weapon;
when he thinks he has found it, he pins the murder on a moll-
ish young woman, Christine Mallory. Rohmer discovers that
both the victim and Wong, the Dunhams' cook, have purple-
stained toes. Rohmer immediately discerns the mysterious hand
of the Orient at work and drags Ballantine to Chinatown to
trace the "Order of the Purple Toes." Van Dine locates a
hobby room in the apartment willed with puzzle boxes and ex-
presses his admiration for publisher Dunham. Dunham, he explains, has the third largest collection of puzzle boxes in
the world. While holding forth on puzzle-box lore, Van Dine
deduces that the murder weapon must be hidden in one of the
boxes. He then proceeds to try to open them all. Chesterton
settles in behind a desk in the study and conducts interviews
with possible witnesses and suspects. When a was figure of
Hyat's secretary is found studded with bodkins, Chesterton
delivers a bit of a speech on voodoo and the belief in the
darker forces.

Narrator Ballantine has a keen sense of humor. He goes
from one writer to the next as the theories of each become too
ridiculous. When the policeman, O'Casey, discovers the murderer, the irony and hilarity of the writers' failure is not
lost on Ballantine. To him, as it is made to seem to us, all
is as it should be. Plodding investigation, not fanciful
theories, is what solves crimes.

This book is a gem in many different ways. It provides

early caricatures of major figures within the genre which are
as apt today as they probably were forty-five years ago. The
prose is as spare and fast moving as Gregory Mcdonald's. There
is an introduction which tells of Ballantine's love of crime
fiction and gives "quotations" from *From Poe to Plethora*.
There is a cast of characters filled with literary and popular
figures of the period, such as Tallulah Bankhead, Robert
Benchley, Stephen Vincent Benet, James M. Cain (as a cook!)
Clifton Fadiman, Dorothy Parker, James Thurber, and Alexander
Woolcott (sic!, "whose name is constantly misspelled." The
book features twelve illustrations which bring to life the
look of the period. You might imagine that you are stepping
into the set of a Fred Astaire film. There are even several
Sinister Orientals. All in all, reading *The Smiling Corpse* is
like entering a time capsule destined for the rich, glossy,
upper-class world of the Thirties. Highly Recommended. (Greg
Goode)

Peter Lovesey. *The Detective Wore Silk Drawers*. Dodd, Mead,
1971, 173 pp.

Sergeant Cribb's first case, *Wobble to Death*, dealt with
race walking; this time, Cribb discovers another odd Victorian
sport--bare-knuckle boxing. The "detective" of the title is
not Cribb, but Henry Jago, sent undercover by Cribb as a boxer
to infiltrate a secret boxing academy and learn who is behind
a series of murders that left headless men to float belly-up
on the Thames. Lovesey is at his best here, using thorough,
solid research of the Victorian era to underlay a well-paced
plot. Lovesey is not a novelist of the first rank, but he is
definitely a cool and competent entertainer who deserves more
attention. (B) (Martin Morse Wooster)

Peter Lovesey. *Waxwork*. Pantheon, 1978, 240 pp.

The editor of this journal has stated that he admires the
Lovesey novels, with the exception of this book. *Waxwork* is
indeed a different sort of book than the other Cribb novels;
where the earlier Cribbs were relatively straightforward novels
of detection, laced with Lovesey's extensive research into
Victorian social history, *Waxwork* tries to be something more,
a compact tragedy of inverted detection, as Cribb tries to un-
cover evidence that will prevent Miriam Cromer from being
executed.
The chief attraction of earlier Cribb novels are the side-
lights Lovesey throws on the past; Lovesey has previously attacked his themes with a sort of infectious brio. The enthusiasm of Lovesey's earlier works is lacking here; all we get
are some dour looks at photography and executions. Lovesey
abandons his strong suits here and tries to do a character
study, but his talents for characterization have always been
weak. *Waxwork*, then, is a competent, sour mess by a writer
who has done better. (C) (Martin Morse Wooster)

Ellery Queen, ed. *Ellery Queen's 1961 Anthology*. Davis,
1960, 320 pp.

Although this series has undergone a long decline in the 1970's, during the 1960's Queen managed to reprint some entertaining, and occasionally excellent, crime fiction. The three novelets this time around are Philip Wylie's "Ten Thousand Blunt Instruments," about murder in the American Museum of Natural History; Georges Simenon's "A Matter of Life and Death," *not* about Maigret but a similar French inspector, who tracks down the cause of a series of murders taking place on a Parisian Christmas; and Hugh Pentecost's "A Matter of Justice," a grim tale of survival in the woods of upstate New York. Other fine stories in this volume are by John Dickson Carr, Lord Dunsany (in one of his rare appearances as a mystery writer), Gerald Kersh, Stanley Ellin, and Budd Schulberg. A choice collection worth searching out. (B+) (Martin Morse Wooster)

Ellery Queen, ed. *Ellery Queen's Anthology*. Volume 41. Davis, 1981, 285 pp.

The latest piece from the EQMM sausage factory is much the same as earlier volumes. The longest story in the volume is a "32,000 word short novel" by Hugh Pentecost, "The Dark Saga." This is actually a collection of five short stories dealing with Jason Dark and his war of vengeance against the Quadrant Corporation, an evil corporation whose sole goal in life appears to be being nasty and bumping off Jason Dark. To paraphrase George Kelley, Pentecost "lacks basic political awareness"; he applies the techniques of the pulp novelist to modern international intrigue, which is rather like chasing a bullet train with a trolley. A major disappointment, and Queen would have been well advised to have reprinted another of the John Smith novellas from the Forties, which were both better written and more entertaining than anything Pentecost is now capable of producing.
As for the short stories, they turn out to be major disappointments as well. Two out of the three best writers EQMM has at this time are present, both with flops: Joyce Harrington with a routine tale of unease, and Patricia Highsmith with a peculiar story told from the viewpoint of a camel. (For the record, the third best writer EQMM has at this time is Ruth Rendell.) The best stories of an admittedly bad lot are by H.G. Wells, oddly enough, and Francis M. Nevins, Jr., a writer who can make the intricacies of copyright law actually appear appealing. A predictable failure from a bankrupt series. (D) (Martin Morse Wooster)

John Buchan. *The Three Hostages*. Houghton Mifflin, 1924, 367 pp.

The fourth Richard Hannay novel is of a different tone than its three predecessors. Hannay, now with a wife and son, is called out of retirement to rescue three children kidnapped by Dominick Medina, a master criminal with plans to rule the world. Although Hannay travels, among other places, to the fjords of Norway and the moors of Scotland, this novel is much more introspective than earlier novels, filled with the stench of a decaying order. As is usual with Buchan novels, the book

44

is well written, if lethargic, worth reading but much less exciting than *The Thirty-Nine Steps* or *Greenmantle*. (B) (Martin
Morse Wooster)

Agatha Christie. *The Seven Dials Mystery*. Dodd, Mead, 1929.

One of Dame Agatha's more obscure novels, concerning the
antics of Bright Young Things Jimmy Thesiger and "Bundle"
Brent, two bored rich aesthetes who have nothing better to do
than be crime fighters, battling the mysterious Seven Dials
Society, an organization that plans to conquer the world (WARN-
ING) through a secret process of hardening wire. (Christie
was not known for her devotion to science.) I've heard this
novel described as being a light and fluffy romp, but in truth
it is an odd hybrid, as if P.G. Wodehouse wrote a spy novel.
The jokes don't hold up too well after fifty years, and *The
Seven Dials Mystery* is merely an account of silly people doing
silly things. Avoid. (D) (Martin Morse Wooster)

John D. MacDonald. *The Quick Red Fox*. Fawcett, 1964, 160 pp.
Bright Orange for the Shroud. Fawcett, 1965, 190 pp.

These are two of the numerous Travis McGee books. In *The
Quick Red Fox* McGee helps a little red-headed actress keep her
secret about a certain wild party which turned into a sex orgy
from ruining her career. The first paragraph contains such a
tantalizing morsel of descriptive prose that I reread it just
to savor the portrayal:

It picked up gray slabs of the Atlantic and smacked them down on
the public beach across the highway from Bahia Mar. It rattled
loose sand across the windshields of the traffic, came into the
cramped acres of docks and boat basin, snapped the burgees and
went *hoooo* in the spiderwebs of rigging and tuna towers.

In *Bright Orange for the Shroud*, an assortment of rapacious
confidence men and a vampirish woman have bled one of McGee's
friends, Arthur Wilkinson, of everything--money, mind, and
manhood--until he is abashed to speak above a whisper and is
ashamed to call himself a human being. When he stumbles up to
the *Busted Flush* he looks like a dog "in countries where they
kick dogs" and collapses on the deck.
My liking *Bright Orange for the Shroud* better than *The
Quick Red Fox* has nothing to do with color preference. First,
the solution to *The Quick Red Fox* is not right. The motiva-
tion is inadequate and the culpability of the culprit is not
credible. I still do not believe that this person did it, not
for a second. The other reason is that the people in this
story are not as interesting and likeable as those in *The
Quick Red Fox*. Not even McGee.
About two-thirds of the way through, *Bright Orange for the
Shroud* ceases to be a mystery and becomes a tale of retribution and justice. Nevertheless, except for the fact that one
of the principal villains escapes scot-free, the outcome is
very pleasing.
Strictly speaking, McGee is not a detective nor an investigator, and, as far as I know, he has never claimed to be,

although most readers of his ventures probably deem him such. Actually, he is just exactly and precisely what he keeps saying he is, a knight in slightly tarnished armor. After reading several of the books, I am inclined to strike out the word "slightly." But, be that as it may, in each of his undertakings McGee is an up-dated knight errant rescuing somebody in distress. One of his adventures would stand up to close correlation to the dominant movements of a chivalrous romance of the Middle Ages. He does not set out to solve a mystery, but to rescue someone requiring a knight.

I found in *Bright Orange for the Shroud* probably as straightforward a statement of MacDonald's philosophy on the male-female sex relation as I have seen:

> It is a bed rhythm, strangely akin to a heart beat ... whum-fa, whum-fa, whum-fa. As eternal, clinical, inevitable as the slow gallop of the heart itself. And as basic to the races, reaching from percale back to the pallet of dried grasses in the cave corner.... Heard even in its most shoddy context, as through the papery walls of a convention motel, this life-beat could be diminished not to evil but to a kind of pathos, because then it was an attempt at affirmation between strangers, a way to try to stop all the clocks, a way to say: I live.... The billions and billions of lives which have come and gone ... came of this life-pulse, and to deny it dignity would be to diminish the blood and need and purpose of the race, make us all bawdy clowns, thrusting and bumping away in a ludicrous heat, shamed by our own instincts.

Somehow this noble sentiment seems to translate within the Travis McGee series into meaning that two weeks in *The Busted Flush*'s master stateroom abed with McGee will put sparkle back into the life of any woman who has given up hope and is almost certain to cure her physically, mentally, and emotionally and get her back on the path of wholesome, stable, vibrant living.

"He was just another symbol of what she had to keep killing, over and over," the deceptively warm and kindly acting confidence man who headed the whole vicious cold-hearted operation told Travis McGee, who replied, "That's one of the shticks of the half-educated, this bite-sized psychiatry, Stebber." Once, after reading six of MacDonald's novels in a row, I felt like saying the same thing about him, because one of my few complaints against him is his need to stop his story while he makes this character and that undergo "ordeal by the psychologist's couch."

Another of my complaints is that all the people in the McGee books, male and female, are just variations of McGee. Their hang-ups, desires, problems, likes, and dislikes are merely McGee altered. I doubt with a deal of earnestness that MacDonald can create a truly cultured, high-classed character.

That MacDonald does write as brilliantly in spurts and snatches as any writer who ever described a shadow waiting in a dark alley to commit mayhem is unarguable. However, side by side with this surpassing workmanship are reams of mediocre story-telling. Explain it? No, I cannot. I only have two partial maybe-explanations: one is that it is difficult for any writer to sustain output at a high level, especially when the output is large; the other is that MacDonald could be a deeply cynical man, and the extra effort required to excell

constantly in a decadent and changing world may not appear
worth it to him. (Frank Floyd)

Frank Gruber. *Swing Low, Swing Dead*. Belmont, 1964.

It is a vast, vast switch to read the sixth number in the
Travis McGee series and then turn immediately to a Johnny
Fletcher mystery. On the one hand, John D. MacDonald dabbles
and interweaves shades of waning light with lines of receding
darkness. Clearly not in the picture are any blotches of pure
yellow warm sunshine. But Frank Gruber, on the other hand,
never kneads other than the merest gently humorous gray into
his clear sunny sky.
    MacDonald, in setting and characterization, is to my know-
ledge the most realistic of today's mystery writers--plot,
situations, action, and other elements of fiction excepted,
certainly. Travis McGee harbors *The Busted Flush* in a tartish-
sweet world, where his friends are cynics or bohemians or both
(McGee himself is a pessimist, like the god Pan frolicking and
fluting), where the villains are hard and knowing and hedon-
istic (or perhaps selfish and greedy and mentally warped), and
where the victims are weak, debilitated, naive, often ex-lushes
still keeping warmed up.
    Far different is Johnny Fletcher's carnival-like blithe-
someness and amateurish spiel, his phony Charlie Chaplin
friends and foes, and the whole train of hammy incidents and
gags, reminiscent of the twenties, recalling *Black Mask* stories
and, among others, the earlier Erle Stanley Gardner good-guy
con artists.
    Before I mislead everyone, I want to go on record as say-
ing that the Johnny Fletcher story, taken for what it is intended to be--entertainment--is good reading. Frank Gruber's
style is very simple, ver-r-y, yet almost flawless--not quite;
the wording is simple, the telling is as simple as the wording.
Gruber would dispose of a murder in a half-dozen lines that
MacDonald would agonize over for nearly as many pages.
    Johnny Fletcher is a fairly smooth and intelligent opera-
tor, but mostly what he has is ingenuity. So what? Everyone
else is more gullable than a nine-month-old chimpanzee. Sam
Cragg, who is Johnny's sidekick and muscular partner, pops
chains in two by flexing his muscles so that Johnny can sell
the little how-to book *Every Man a Samson*. Sam is just brawny,
not brainy. He defends his eye-sight--"My eyes are thirty-
thirty." On being called Fletcher's confederate, Sam feels
misrepresented: "Confederate?" he exclaims, "I'm a Yankee."
    Swing Low, Swing Dead is fast-paced from the start (when
Sam wins a plagerized song in a hotel crap game) to finish,
and the solution is satisfying, except in four slight details.
Read with an uncritical eye, it provides fun and adventure
with Johnny and Sam. Besides being fun, it is also built on
a pretty sound mystery foundation. (Frank Floyd)

Hilary Watson, ed. *Winter's Crimes 12*. MacMillan, 1980.
Herbert Harris, ed. *John Creasey's Crime Collection 1981*.
    Gollancz, 1981. Published in the U.S. by St. Martin's.

    Britain's two annual crime anthologies of note. The Mac-

Millan volume has twelve stories, all original. The Gollancz
volume has sixteen, but only five are original. Each cast
list is star-studded, but only Michael Gilbert (writing one
original and one reprint) features in both.

It has been three or four months since I read these two
books, and the acid test of time reveals that the MacMillan is
the more even collection (no real losers) while the Gollancz
boasts the most memorable story (P.D. James's "A Very Commonplace Murder") and the least comprehensive (Ernest Dudley's
"Chinatown Cowboy"). The Gollancz also has neat little vi-
gnettes from Christiana Brand (reprint) and Colin Watson
(original) and a disappointing entry from H.R.F. Keating.

There's really not a lot to chose between them, and so
many good authors. Buy both. (Bob Adey)

(Continued from page 37) "Nameless" novel cobbled together out
of disconnected short stories and no "Nameless" novel at all,
I'll make the cobbled choice every time. There is a humanity
about the P.I. which comes through in the books--all the books
--and makes them eminently readable, whatever they may lack in
cohesiveness. This is especially true of *Scattershot*. There
is another thing about it which deserves comment as well.
Pronzini has accomplished a great deal for one so young, and,
at least from what one can tell from public aspects of his
career, he has not had much experience coping with failure.
Nevertheless, when he writes about his P.I. doing all the
right things for all the right reasons and *still* taking it on
the chops, this reader at least is left with the feeling that
Pronzini knows what it's like from personal experience. If he
is drawing from his own experiences, he is to be commended for
the skill with which he communicates those feelings to his
readers; if he is inventing it all out of whole cloth, he is
to be congratulated on possessing a world-class imagination of
striking perception. Either way, it's a fine performance. The
ending of *Scattershot* won't make you happy--it's not intended
to--but you won't close this book without being moved.

PARTING SHOTS

If you've stayed with me all the way, chasing through the
pages of this issue, I congratulate you on your tenacity and
persistence. Just a few more comments should fill up this
page and thus eliminate the last vestige of white space from
the entire magazine. You will notice that Walter Albert's
movie column, for which there has been some demand, makes its
debut in this issue, accompanied by a "More Movie Reviews"
department contributed entirely by Jim Traylor this time out.
Walter's column will be a permanent feature; "More Movie Reviews" will appear, or not, as interest and material dictates.

The letters column is especially spare this time out, and
I hope you people will soon return to your usual verbose and
argumentative ways. I suspect that Bill Loeser may lead the
charge in the next issue. He was slow renewing his subscription this year, and when he sees the article on comics in the
last issue and the two columns on movies in this one, he may
be jolted from the silence he has observed for too long.

The Documents
In the Case

Letters

From Steve Schultheis, 7529 Carlisle Way, Goleta, CA 93117:
I've greatly enjoyed the November/December issue of *The Mystery Fancier*, and I am glad to be back on the subscription list once again. Everything in the issue was good, and it's hard to say one item was better than another, but I *did* get the most pleasure (in chuckles) out of "Doctor Wonderful." I dearly love the old pulps *and* Nancy Drew and spunky female sleuths of the old school in general, and Dr. Nancy Dayland must have combined the worst traits of the whole bunch. Delightful!

From Greg Goode, 50 Washburn Park, Rochester, NY 14620:
First, let me correct what I said in my l.o.c. in TMF 6:1 about "The Two Quick Devils of Totsuka." It is a picaresque chase story set in Japan about two American teenagers trying to escape after having taken a photograph of the Mikado; it is not about Japanese adventurers. Sorry.
Although you do not want to print too many complimentary remarks about TMF, please let me say that I like the glossy cover and the book review index. Not having seen enough back issues, I don't know whether the index is a regular feature; if it has not been, I hope it becomes one. [*It has been a regular feature from the beginning. Jeff Meyerson did the index to volume one, which appeared in TMF 2:1. David Doerrer has done all the subsequent indexes, which have appeared in 3:1, 4:2, 5:2, and, of course, 6:1. Indexing anything is a difficult and often thankless task, and I take this opportunity to again thank Jeff and David for their work.*]
Enjoyed K. Arne Blom's article on comic strip detectives! As (he? she? [*Arne is a he. He is also a prolific Swedish mystery writer, one of whose books is slated to be released by Raven House in the next year or two (in an English translation, of course).*]) says, the comic strip is primarily a visual medium. Critics who love using the words "terse" and "lean" for P.I. stories might probably run out of skinny adjectives when it comes to comic strip P.I. tales. Incidentally, the book *Dick Tracy*, by William Johnston (Tempo Books, 1970), is a novelization of a Dick Tracy comic strip story in which Mr. Tracy battles Mr. Computer. It reads like a comic strip looks and reads. Does anyone know whether there have been any original detectives in Big Little Books?
Also enjoyed Dick Wenstrup's comments on David Byrd's

cover art for the Warner Max Brand books. I looked through
several art and artist indexes and bibliographies but couldn't
find David Byrd's name anywhere. [*See Carol Brener's letter
below.*] Other publishers are also doing tasteful covers which
evoke a 30's-40's feeling. Vintage has some very good cinema-
style art deco covers for Manuel Puig's "detective novels."
The art is signed by Topazio. Pantheon has just come out with
a series of nice covers in their "international" series. I
think the cover to Dickinson's book *The Poison Oracle* is the
best--at least it is the most bizarre. And Avon has some
period covers which look so much like the Harper Perennial
covers that I have been fooled for a few seconds on several
occasions. The books are a series by Lionel Black.

From Carol Brener, Murder Ink, 271 W. 87th St., New York, NY:
     In answer to Dick Wenstrup's query about artist David Byrd:
     1) He did all the "new" Avon Dorothy L. Sayers covers.
     2) He did the cover for (non-mystery) *Bijou* by David Mad-
        den.
     3) He did the posters for *Godspell* and *Follies*--shows--and
        others. (See the large trade paperback on the history
        of U.S. poster art.)
     I think he's great! Some of his original artwork (for the
Sayers cover, and posters) is for sale at Good Company Gallery,
339 Columbus Ave., New York City. (That's at 75th Street, and
the telephone number is 212/724-7244.)

From Ev Bleiler, somewhere in the wilds of New Jersey:
     I am enclosing an article on an early crime novel, which,
so far as I know, has never been described, though it is listed
in Hubin.
     I also have a question for your letter column, for those
of your readers who know more about motion pictures than I do.
     Last night I happened to see an old Sherlock Holmes pic-
ture, *A Study in Scarlet* (World-Wide Films, 1933), which, as
might be expected, had nothing to do with Doyle's book of the
same title except that it concerned two gentlemen named Sherlock Holmes and Dr. Watson, with, intermittently, a Scotland
Yard man named Lestrade (pronounced Less-strayed).
     It was a lousy picture, but it contained two of three ele-
ments that are basic to Agatha Christie's *And Then There Were
None,* which was first published in 1938, five years later.
     The basic situation was a tontine, in which members were
assassinated to the accompaniment of little notes about so-
many little black boys, and then there were so-many little
black boys less one. And the murderer achieved his fell purpose by himself feigning to be assassinated, with the conniv-
ance of another of the potential victims.
     Has anyone ever written this up or commented on this? Ac-
cording to DeWaal's *World Bibliography of Sherlock Holmes and
Dr. Watson,* the screen play was written by Robert Florey,
about whom I know nothing. Does anyone know if this associa-
tion of two motifs--ten little Indians, falsified death--was
original with Florey? Did Christie ever make any comment
about the movie or Florey?

From Bob Adey, 7 Highcroft Ave., Wordsley, Stourbridge, West
Midlands, DY8 5LX, ENGLAND:
     So you can't read my writing, you [*here follows a group of*

five or six illegible words]. Anyone among your readers who remembers that very nice man, Berry Johns, will know that you have paid me no mean compliment to put me in Berry's league; Ah, those quotes when you knew Berry had got something good for you, but you couldn't make out what it was.

David Doerrer will not find a Callan book called "File on a Willing Victim." As Barry Van Tilberg noted, this Callan item is in *The Bell House Book*, an anthology celebrating the sixtieth anniversary of a literary agency. The Mitchell story is of about short-story length only and is a reprint from the *Sunday Express*, circa 1972, where I understand that a number of Callan shorts appeared about that time. Incidentally, *The Bell House Book* was dated 1979.

I don't know whether to be pleased or not that the discerning Charlie Shibuk has highlighted the apparent excellence of Howard Rigsby's paperback original, *Lucinda*. I say apparent because I've never yet managed to lay hands on a copy since I first read the same Boucher review to which Charlie referred. A very elusive lady, our Lucinda.

I'll enclose a few more reviews and conclude by saying how interesting I found Bob Sampson's article on the embryonic police procedural series.

From Barry Van Tilburg, 4380 67th Ave. N., Pinellas Park, FL:
Am eagerly awaiting next issue of TMF. Here's another installment of my spy series characters in hardback. I am contemplating (only contemplating) doing an article on spy series in paperback in the same format as the one in hardback.

P.S. For anyone interested, here is an update on Dossier #15: Quiller. *The Pekin Target*, by Adam Hall (Collins, L7.50).

[*From a later note:*]
Really loved TMF 6/1. The reviews were good, but the best part was "The Detective Hero in Comics" by K. Arne Blom. In comic book form my favorite was Nick Fury.

There are some great movies on now. I've seen "Death Wish II," Robert Littell's "The Amateur," and am planning on seeing Agatha Christie's "Evil Under the Sun" with Peter Ustinov recreating his role as Hercule Poirot.

Due to a screw-up (probably mine) there was an error in Dossier #52. All books are listed properly, but the publisher of the hardbacks was Howard Baker. The first ones listed are paperback edition listings.

[*The screw-up was mine, as usual. Since the name of the publisher was the same as that of the author, I assumed that the hard-covers were a self-publishing venture on Baker's part. Why that should have bothered me I am now at a loss to explain, but bother me it did so I looked the books up in Hubin's Bibliography and discovered several discrepancies. You had, for example, listed* Destination Dieppe *as being published by Howard Baker in 1967, while Hubin shows it as having been published by Mayflower in 1965. Mayflower being a paperback house, and your series being about series in hardback, I ought to have left the entries alone, but my weakness for wanting to cite the first appearance got the best of me and I made the changes, which also resulted in a reshuffling of the order in which the books are listed. Per your original MS, the first four entries should have read:* The Dirty Game *(Howard Baker, 1967);* Destination Dieppe *(Howard Baker, 1967);* The Girl, the City, and the Soldier *(Howard Baker, 1968);* The Night of the Wolfe *(Howard Baker, 1969). Sorry.*]

www.ingramcontent.com/pod-product-compliance
Lightning Source LLC
Chambersburg PA
CBHW031616040426

42452CB00006B/544